DAILY LIFE IN COLONIAL AMERICA

VENERATE THE PLOUGH

DAILY LIFE

IN

COLONIAL AMERICA

Reader's Digest

THE READER'S DIGEST ASSOCIATION, INC.
Pleasantville, New York/Montreal

VIRGINIA PLANTATION

SPANISH CAVALRYMAN

NEW YORK COFFEE HOUSE

DAILY LIFE IN COLONIAL AMERICA
Edited and designed by Media Projects Incorporated

Executive Editor: C. Carter Smith
Project Editor: Edith Alston
Managing Editor: Lelia Wardwell
Art Director: Harakawa Sisco Inc.
Production Editor: Sara Colacurto

CONTRIBUTORS
Principal Writer: Ogden Tanner
Writers: Zane Kotker, Kevin Osborn, Ann Weil,
    Charles A. Wills

RESEARCHERS
Shelley Latham, Stephanie Rabinowitz, Anne Wright

READER'S DIGEST STAFF
Editor: James Cassidy
Art Editor: Evelyn Bauer
Art Associate: Martha Grossman

READER'S DIGEST GENERAL BOOKS
Editor in Chief: John A. Pope, Jr.
Managing Editor: Jane Polley
Executive Editor: Susan J. Wernert
Art Director: David Trooper
Group Editors: Will Bradbury, Sally French,
    Norman B. Mack, Kaari Ward
Group Art Editors: Evelyn Bauer, Robert M. Grant,
    Joel Musler
Chief of Research: Laurel A. Gilbride
Copy Chief: Edward W. Atkinson
Picture Editor: Richard Pasqual
Rights and Permissions: Pat Colomban
Head Librarian: Jo Manning

Overleaf: The Old State House, Boston, by James Brown Marston
Half title: Engraving from *Columbian Magazine*

PICTURE CREDITS
Front cover: *clockwise from top left; for key to abbreviations see p. 144:* LC;
Museum of Fine Arts, Boston; LC (2); CW; NPS; LC
Back cover: *clockwise from top left; for key to abbreviations see p. 144:*
NPS (2); Holland Society of NY; YCHS; CW; Rhode Island School of Design

The credits and acknowledgments that appear on page 144 are
hereby made a part of this copyright page.

Library of Congress Cataloging in Publication Data
    Daily life in colonial America / [designed and edited by Media
    Projects, Inc.].
        p. cm. — (Journeys into the past)
    Includes index.
    ISBN 0-89577-497-6
    1. United States—Social life and customs—Colonial period, ca.
    1600–1775. I. Media Projects Incorporated. II. Series.
    E162.D16 1993
    973.2—dc20   93-2719

CONTENTS

1788 PARADE BANNER

PENNSYLVANIA FRAKTUR CERTIFICATE

NEW ORLEANS CITY PLAN

MAP OF COASTAL VIRGINIA

THE PEOPLES OF AMERICA

The Native Americans inhabited what the Europeans termed

"the new golden land." Hungry for land and wealth, these settlers were to establish a diverse

and extraordinary nation—unfortunately at the expense of the first Americans.

ANTHROPOLOGISTS TELL US that the first people to reach the continental Americas were a band of hunters from Siberia, who arrived during one of the Ice Ages many thousands of years ago. These people crossed into what is now Alaska at a time when so much water was frozen into glaciers that the sea level was lowered, and the Bering Strait was dry land.

By the time Columbus arrived, it is estimated that the population of these first Americans had expanded to several million people living within the present boundaries of the United States. Some were farmers and some were hunter-gatherers. Agriculture based on corn, beans, and squash had spread from Mexico into the American Southwest, up the Mississippi Valley, and throughout the forests of the East Coast. Some Native Americans lived in villages or groups of villages with a few hundred residents; still others were organized into affiliated towns or small states of a few thousand citizens. Their different societies had developed more than 200 languages.

Then the Europeans came.

THE GREAT EXPERIMENT

They came in successive waves from many cultural backgrounds during the colonial era—Spanish, French, English, Dutch, German, Swedish, Scottish, Irish, and more. Each group helped shape a new civilization on the continent they called the New World, and each left its special mark.

Among the first were soldier-explorers sent to claim new territory and riches for their kings, accompanied by missionaries seeking new converts for the Christian God. As the tide of immigration mounted, however, most who came to America were ordinary citizens: farmers, laborers, shopkeepers, and artisans. A high proportion were indentured servants who agreed to work off their contracts in return for sea passage; many, considered the dregs of Europe, were convicts, debtors, and drifters pressed into service by enterprising promoters who wanted to swell the ranks for their money-making settlement schemes.

Many others came for reasons of religious conviction, including Pilgrims, Puritans, and Quakers dissenting from the Church of England, as well as French Huguenots (Protestants), German Lutherans from Salzburg and Moravia, and Spanish Jews, all fleeing repression by the Roman Catholic Church in their homelands. For those bold enough to grasp it, the New World was an unprecedented opportunity, a place where anyone could seek the land, the liberty, and the wealth that had been denied him by the old order at home. At the same time, the very act of going there was a leap of faith, a great experiment, a gamble not suited to the faint of heart.

What they all found on arrival—after long, miserable voyages across the Atlantic, during which many sickened or died—was like

CLIFF DWELLING The Mesa Verde Indians built this pueblo in a canyon wall of what is now Colorado in about 1100 A.D. The site was abandoned around 1275, possibly as a result of warfare or drought.

EUROPEANS ON THE HUDSON Henry Hudson, exploring for the Dutch, sailed up the river that would one day bear his name. The Indians greeted him and traded beaver and otter skin for beads, knives, and hatchets.

nothing they had ever known before. Compared to the small, crowded, authoritarian nations they had left behind, North America was in many ways wide open for the taking. But the continent was not simply the glorious new Eden that pro-

SEASHELL GORGET This finely engraved decorative neck piece was made by Native Americans from what is now southeastern Tennessee. It has an abstract spider and circle motif worked into its design.

moters had presented it to be. This Eden was also a vast, forbidding land.

"What could they see but a hideous and desolate wilderness, full of wild beasts and wild men," wrote William Bradford of his fellow Pilgrims who disembarked at Plymouth. "[And] if they looked behind them there was the mighty ocean.... What could now sustain them but the Spirit of God and His grace?"

In such surroundings, a settler first had to hold off starvation, and a prudent one carried his musket with him wherever he went. An even more useful companion was his ax. In most areas along the Eastern seaboard the land was tall and darkly forested, unlike the settled parts of Europe, where most trees had long ago been cut down. The forest was, first of all, an obstacle that had to be cleared for farming—a back-breaking task. But it was also a boon, supplying the

7

settlers with countless raw materials to build and heat their homes; to make their tools, plows, and fences; to fashion furniture, barrels, and eating implements; to construct the fishing boats and merchant ships that provided seacoast settlements with their livelihoods. Colonial America, indeed, was a society built on wood. Its warm grain, its sweet smell, and its cheerful crackling in the fireplace sustained many colonists in their darkest hours—and those images still linger in the American soul.

Chronologically, the story of colonial America did not begin with the celebrated Pilgrims of Plymouth, or even the earlier, star-crossed pioneers of Jamestown, but many years before, with the Spanish conquistadors on the coast of

CULTURES CLASH
This engraving, from Captain John Smith's *Generall Historie of Virginia,* shows the leader of the Jamestown colony taking Chief Powhatan prisoner. Relations between these two men were often tense as the needs of the Indians and the English came into conflict.

SETTLING IN The successful building of log cabins, as shown above, was perfected by Swedish settlers in the Delaware River Valley, where there were abundant forests. These had to be cleared before the settlers could begin living off the land. The painting at left, by folk artist Edward Hicks, depicts William Penn, founder of Pennsylvania, trading with the Delaware Indians and presenting them with a treaty. In 1681, Penn established a fair system for land transactions and trade relations between the Indians and the colonists.

PENNS TREATY with the INDIANS.made 1681 with out an Oath.and never broken.The foundation of Religious and Civil LIBERTY.in the U.S. of AMERICA.

Florida. Geographically, settlement was not always a push from East to West. *Rancheros,* arriving by way of Mexico, introduced the horses, cattle, sheep, and new agricultural crops that would one day dominate the western American way of life. Another important strand of American culture began with French canoemen, the colorful *coureurs de bois*, who paddled from the St. Lawrence region deep into the continent to trade for furs—and who, unlike many later Americans, lived in relative harmony with their Indian hosts.

Nor was life in the colonies as idyllic as it is sometimes portrayed. Families often lived in crude and unsanitary conditions, were limited to the most primitive kinds of medicine, and had to get over the tragedy of losing wife, husband, and child after child to epidemic disease. Drinking, gambling, fighting, and adultery were common. Condemnation of crimes could be swift and public, however, and punishment was commonly administered with the whip or, in extreme cases, the noose. Discipline was especially cruel against those who were considered of lesser social status and who had to be "kept in line": slaves, Indians, servants, and, quite often, children and wives.

Nevertheless, a remarkable spirit of cooperation sprang up among those who had cast their lots together in the new land. It was the outstanding feature of frontier settlements, noted by foreign travelers throughout the colonial period. Neighbors turned out for miles around to help struggling newcomers build their cabins, raise their barns, or bring in their first crops.

The land itself posed challenges that shaped a new kind of American. While colonists tried wherever they could to reproduce the European surroundings with which they were familiar, they also learned much from neighboring Native Americans. They picked up many tricks of hunting and fishing; they adopted the use of moccasins, snowshoes, and canoes; they learned the properties of various herbs as medicines, and the practice of girdling and burning trees to create farmland; they followed Indian techniques of planting corn, squash, pumpkins, and other native staples, without which most early colonists would never have survived. In the Jamestown colony planters also discovered an Indian crop called tobacco, which, with the help of slaves

NEW ENGLAND WEDDING **This richly detailed embroidery, crafted by an anonymous settler, depicts a wedding, thought to be that of Hannah Green and Gardinier Chandler in 1755. The friends and family members arrive and gather with the minister outside the church.**

The Gablent, Fronting George Street,
It was Build In the year, 1753,
And the Old log-Church taken Away,
It Stud at the Same place.

Dr. Rouse

old School house

THE NEW REPUBLIC By the end of the 18th century, many towns in the eastern United States looked very much like small towns in Europe. This watercolor by folk artist Lewis Miller shows the Old Stone Church in York, Pennsylvania.

the steepled New England village with its central common, the adobe mission and plaza of the Southwest and California, and the graceful Georgian mansion of the plantation South.

Our American forebears came here from several continents and many nations. Their languages, customs, and religious traditions were extremely diverse. But, they had in common the desire and grit to make a better life in the new land.

In his *Letters from an American Farmer*, the French-born colonist, Hector St. John de Crèvecoeur, summed up that most compelling of notions:

"We have no princes for whom we toil, starve, and bleed: we are the most perfect society now existing in the world.... It is of very little importance how, and in what manner a ... man arrives; for if he is but sober, honest, and industrious, he has nothing more to ask of heaven. Let him go to work, he will have opportunities enough.... There is room for everybody in America.... Here man is free as he ought to be....

"Here individuals of all nations are melted into a new race of men, whose labours and posterity will one day cause great changes in the world."

Daily Life in Colonial America surveys the everyday experiences, trials, and triumphs of the different groups of people who crossed the Atlantic Ocean to the New World to establish colonies and, ultimately, a separate nation of their own. The period covered begins with the first Spanish settlement in Florida in 1565 and concludes with the Louisiana Purchase in 1803, when the United States acquired the last French colonial lands in North America.

imported from Africa, built the plantation economy of the South. Ironically, slavery was introduced at Jamestown the same year (1619) that the first representative government in the colonies was founded. This was the Virginia House of Burgesses, which granted its members the right to vote on issues relating to the Jamestown settlement.

In adapting to their new lives, the settlers produced much of which they could be proud. The fruits of American ingenuity ranged from the Conestoga wagon, the Kentucky long rifle, and the cotton gin, to the fine furniture of Philadelphia cabinetmakers and the exquisite creations of silversmiths like Paul Revere. Among the most memorable achievements in building are such distinctive regional trademarks as

For God, Gold, and Glory

18TH-CENTURY SPANISH FRONTIER SOLDIER

Beginning in the 16th century, Spanish conquistadors and holy

men moved north from the Caribbean and Mexico to expand their New World empire

and spread the Catholic faith. Over the next 200 years they would create

new ways of life from Florida to California, introducing horses, sheep, and cattle

ranching, and new crops like oranges, olives, and wheat.

When Spanish rule ended the land was infused with elements of culture, language,

and blood that still course through America's veins.

Spain's First Foothold

In the shoreline garrison town of St. Augustine, the Spanish divided their

energies between establishing a secured settlement and converting the native Indian population

to Catholicism. The Spanish intermarried with natives, creating new cultural groups.

O N SEPTEMBER 8, 1565, five ships with 500 soldiers under Don Pedro Menéndez de Avilés dropped anchor in a sheltered harbor 40 miles south of present-day Jacksonville, claiming the land they called La Florida for Spain. The men—along with a number of women settlers—sought temporary refuge in a village of friendly Timucuan Indians, then set about building a wooden fort, which Don Pedro named in honor of the feast day of Saint Augustine, when the land had first been sighted. As a key outpost of Spain's New World empire, the town of St. Augustine would survive centuries of hardship to become the oldest permanent European settlement in the United States.

As the *presidio*, or garrison, grew, small cattle ranches and a string of Franciscan missions were built inland, but they proved no match for hostile Indian tribes and marauding English forces, which occasionally sacked the settlement. The worst assault was led by Sir Francis Drake, whose army and fleet of 42 vessels drove out the garrison and burned the town in 1586. In response, the defenders rebuilt, rimming their town with walls of logs and earth, and constructed a massive citadel, the Castillo de San Marcos, into which the population could retreat when under attack. Built of coquina stone, with ramparts up to 30 feet high and 13 feet thick, the castillo proved its worth when an English army from the Carolinas assaulted its

GARRISON TOWN   The walls of the castillo were a constant reminder of St. Augustine's military purpose. The rank of an 18th-century Spanish officer was displayed in the braid on his uniform and lace cuffs. Boys from the black slave population served as regimental drummers, drawing crowds to hear proclamations made on the plaza. The black cassock was the uniform of the parish priest; mission friars wore the garb of their order.

MAJOLICA Spanish potters had been making the tin-glazed earthenware called majolica long before colonization of the New World began. Similar wares, produced in Mexican kilns, replaced the Old World varieties in Florida and the Caribbean. These 18th-century pots came from Puebla, Mexico.

walls in 1702. English cannon pounded vainly at the fort, where some 1,500 residents took refuge, in a siege that lasted six weeks. Finally the invaders gave up, but burned the town as they departed, so that again it had to be rebuilt.

Like all of Spain's New World settlements, St. Augustine was founded with a twofold purpose: to hold the land in the name of the king, and to convert the natives to the Catholic faith. (The Spanish, though often harsh in their treatment of the Indians, believed that converting them saved their souls. The English, in contrast, rarely attempted to convert or educate the natives.) St. Augustine was a town of soldiers and priests, along with their dependents: wives, children, servants, Indian converts, and merchants and artisans who served their needs. Because of its strategic location on important sea lanes connecting Europe and the New World, the colony was subsidized by the Spanish crown. All who lived there depended on the *situado*, the government payroll sent by ship from Mexico City, capital of New Spain. When the situado was late—as it often was, by months or even years—all citizens, regardless of rank, had to tighten their belts.

THE NAME OF LA FLORIDA

The discoverer of Florida, Juan Ponce de León, named the peninsula he thought was an island in honor of the day he first came ashore, Easter Sunday, in 1513. Pascua Florida is the Spanish name for the religious holiday.

LIFE AROUND THE PLAZA

Though the castillo dominated the town, the focus of community life, as in other 18th-century Spanish settlements, was its spacious central plaza, a gathering place and parade ground open on one side to the harbor. Around other sides were the governor's house, other public buildings, and shops. Near the plaza, along narrow, shady streets, stood the private houses and walled gardens of the high-ranking officials, known as *peninsulares* because they came from the Iberian peninsula of mainland Spain. Since few Spanish ladies journeyed to such a remote outpost, these men generally found wives in the New World.

Prosperous families ate fish and venison served on imported majolica tableware, and drank Spanish wine out of Spanish goblets. Ladies cooled themselves with ivory fans and carried parasols against the hot sun, modestly covering their heads and faces—all but one eye—with long black *mantillas*, or shawls. In many upper-class households, Indian women or black slaves took care of the children, tended the gardens, cooked, and performed other tasks.

A step down in rank from the peninsulares were the *criollos*, men of Spanish descent who had been born in the New World (where the enervating climate was thought to have rendered them inferior to men born in Spain). Though they accounted for a majority of the population, they could rarely aspire to the highest political and military offices—a source of resentment against their supposed superiors. Like peninsulares, most criollos married *criollas*, women of Spanish descent born in the town or elsewhere in New Spain. Some ran stores, selling imported sugar, rum, spices, utensils, fabrics, buttons, and tobacco, which both men and women smoked in hand-rolled cigars. In their leisure time, the men of St. Augustine might enjoy a cockfight or horse race, or repair to a local *taberna* to drink wine or sugar-cane

TOOL FOR TEACHING A trio of devils carries a sinner off to Hell in this woodcut used by missionaries to frighten Indians into conversion.

brandy. Some tabernas were considered respectable enough for escorted ladies; others were places for dancing to lively music, gambling, or playing cards. Soldiers newly arrived from Spain were welcomed for the latest dances they could teach: the *fandango* from Andalucía, the *jota* from Aragón, or the odd *meona*, in which dancers formed a ring and simultaneously squirted mouthfuls of water into the center. At tabernas that also sold food, garlicky stews were a favorite meal—an *olla podrida* of meat or seafood and vegetables—followed by sugar-coated cakes.

Except for extra tables and chairs and a sign out front, most tabernas resembled middle-class houses. Smaller, and located farther from the plaza than upper-class homes, the houses of the middle class were generally arranged on the same courtyard plan. High walls on three sides—built of coquina or a concrete made from ground oyster shells called tabby—provided privacy from the street and neighbors; roofed porches and balconies gave relief from the sun. More modest houses had only two ground-floor rooms, with small windows; families who prospered would build another room above.

Cooking was done over a fire in the yard, or in a separate kitchen building. Nearby was a household garden, where the owners grew sweet potatoes, lettuce, cabbage, peppers, pumpkins, and watermelons. Oranges, introduced by the Spanish to the New World, were a prized food. Sometimes a housewife took oranges to the market on the plaza to barter with the women from the Guale Indian village outside the town walls for a catfish or for corn to add to her family's stew. She simmered her stews in Guale clay pots like ones found in every St. Augustine home.

At the edges of town, or in the Indian village nearby, lived the humblest families. Many were of mixed blood. *Mulatos* had both white and black ancestors, and *mestizos* were the offspring of Indian and Spanish parents. Blacks were usually slaves. Subsisting on garden crops and the region's game and fish, the families also sold what food they could.

HOME LIFE   A soldier's wife boils grease and lye, distilled from wood ashes, to make a soft soap she will sell as a means of earning extra income for the household. While the son picks oranges from the family's tree, the daughter embroiders a pair of pockets for her mother, who will wear them out of sight under her full skirt. A low covered well lined with stacked barrels supplies the family's water; after a few years the barrels will rot, and a new well will be dug.

RELIGIOUS LIFE IN ST. AUGUSTINE

Tending to the spiritual needs of the community were the holy men of the Catholic Church. The parish priests instructed children of upper-class families, and put on vestments over their black cassocks to say early morning Mass for the townsfolk, or to preside over marriages, baptisms, and funerals. At the south edge of town, Franciscan friars, wearing the hooded blue-gray robes, knotted belts, and sandals of their order, attended to the conversion and religious education of the Indians from their mission compound.

Both priests and friars performed the final rites to conduct the dead of St. Augustine into their graves. Usually, bodies would be placed in a shroud, lowered into the ground, and sprinkled with lime; a leading citizen might be placed in a wooden coffin and buried under the floor of the parish church. But religious concern was with the soul, and in the 18th century death usually brought concern for the body to an end.

The Spanish ruled St. Augustine for more than 200 years. In 1763 they lost it to the British, but regained it 20 years later. In 1821, Florida peacefully became a territory of the United States.

SIMPLE AND SPARE Household furnishings were spartan in colonial Florida, and the few chairs were usually reserved for men. Walls periodically needed a new coat of whitewash, inside and out, because of the region's damp air.

A ROYAL ROAD NORTH

The Spanish frontier depended on a desert trail 1,500 miles long to connect it with

the colonial capital at Mexico City. The trail quickly became an important trade route—and

the path along which Old World ranching entered the American Southwest.

WHILE THEIR BEACHHEAD to the east was being established in Florida, the Spanish also ventured north after their conquest of Mexico, seeking still greater treasures in the Southwest. As early as 1542, lured by Indian tales of gold, a young nobleman named Francisco Vásquez de Coronado had probed as far as the plains of what would become Kansas. He found no gold and no cities—only a vast, barren wilderness dotted with ragged villages of grass shacks or the Indian towns of adobe brick that the Spanish called *pueblos*.

Nevertheless, dreams of conquest persisted. In 1598, when Spain authorized the province of New Mexico, its newly appointed governor, Don Juan de Oñate, set out with 270 soldiers, 130 families, and 7,000 cattle to colonize the territory. Following the Rio Grande north from what is now El Paso, Don Juan established a *camino real*—a "royal road," or "king's highway"—to Santa Fe, a rough outpost that would become the provincial capital.

This dirt trail winding through the desert was more rugged than royal, but it became the lifeline between the frontier and New Spain's capital at Mexico City, 1,500 miles to the south. It guided a steady stream of Spanish soldiers, missionaries, and settlers, bringing herds of horses, cattle, and sheep into the region to establish their colonies and missions in the sparse, arid land of the pueblos.

Travelers along the camino sought safety in numbers against natural hardships and frequent Indian attacks. Would-be colonists might wait for months to join a scheduled caravan of mule- or ox-drawn wagons, defended by mounted soldiers, carrying much-needed supplies and mail up the trail to Santa Fe. For

THE HORSE IN TWO WORLDS

OF ALL THE SPANISH innovations in the New World, none had a more visible impact than the arrival of the horse. Borne across the Atlantic in shipboard slings, the animals were bred on Caribbean and Mexican ranches that followed traditions of horsemanship more than a thousand years old. Spanish soldiers and settlers brought the herds north to open up the American Southwest, and introduced ranch practices—the cattle drive, roundups, cattle branding—that became hallmarks of American life.

American Indians, at first awestruck by the "big dogs," soon discovered that horses could give them vastly greater mobility in hunting—and in striking back at the white men who were invading their ancestral lands. Apaches and Comanches raided Spanish outposts to build their own herds. Above all, the horse made the Plains Indians masters of the buffalo, on which whole tribes based their way of life.

SLINGS AND FETTERS A 1529 drawing shows a means of safely transporting horses by ship.

TERRA INCOGNITA Except for the vastness of the territory, this 1551 map of Spanish exploration conveys more fantasy than fact. Soldiers who actually journeyed into the Southwest put aside the steel armor of the conquistadors in favor of light leather shields. The Spanish sword at right was unearthed in Georgia.

the journey, which might last another three months, they brought their own dried meat and beans, and water casks for the long, dry stretches of road. The hooded wagons bulged with valuable cargoes of arms and ammunition, tools, cooking utensils, window glass, paper, and books. Stocked along with these were fresh supplies of New World products, including sugar, tobacco, wine—and chocolate, which the Spanish had learned about from the Aztecs. The dried beans, packed in leather pouches, were sold for grinding and mixing with hot milk as a luxurious drink.

Along the way, settlers on the ranches waited eagerly to barter their stocks of dried meat, wool, home-woven goods, and tanned hides for the treasures of the caravans. A substantial ranch might incorporate a fortified watchtower in its walls, where the *ranchero* could post a lookout to catch the first sight of dust raised by the train of distant wagons. From the tower roof the sentinel might shout, blow a horn, or bang a drum in greeting—or give out a warning if Indians were about to attack. In the latter case, ranch hands would come running, retreating inside the tower to fire through the narrow slits in the walls at the enemy with crossbows and guns.

LIFE ON THE RANCH

The Spanish ranch house was built of *adobe*, sun-dried bricks of mud and straw, long used by local Pueblo Indians for their own homes, with walls thick enough to keep the interiors cool in summer and warm in winter. The main rooms—sleeping quarters, kitchen, dining room, storerooms, perhaps a special weaving room, a finely furnished guest room, and a small chapel—were arranged around a courtyard, or *placita* (little plaza), which was surrounded by a continuous wall to protect the heart of the ranch against

SPECIAL TREAT Chocolate beans were ground, mixed with sugar and hot milk, and served in special cups, often made of copper, with a stick called a *molinero* for stirring it into a foamy drink. The beans were a luxury item in the caravan trade.

desert winds and Indian attack. On most days, the courtyard, onto which all rooms of the ranch house opened, was the vibrant center of ranch life. In the middle there usually stood a well or fountain, often planted with colorful flowers, around which the women and Indian servants of the ranch could exchange gossip while they filled their water jugs. Against a wall stood one or more *hornos*, beehive-shaped ovens that produced a constant supply of baked goods. The largest kind of oven, called a *papá*, was used to make *dulces*, the sweet-flavored cakes that were favorite treats; a medium-sized *mamá* was for regular breads; and a child-sized *niño* might be used to burn incense to perfume the air. Part of the courtyard was usually shaded by one or more trees, under which workers could rest from their chores and the noonday sun. Set into a wall might be a small shrine to San Isidro, the farmers' patron saint, before which individuals could pause for a moment of prayer.

Close to the house were a chicken coop, goat pen, pig sty, and horse corral—which had a separate enclosure for the ranch's burros, the small, sturdy donkeys that served as work animals and delighted the children as pets. Beyond the outbuildings lay open pastures for grazing cattle and sheep, as well as fields of corn, beans, and wheat, apple and apricot orchards, and a vineyard for producing wine. Irrigation ditches, dug by native ranch hands, and lined with hollowed logs, routed water from a nearby stream to the fields.

A PADRE'S PLAN FOR REFORM

66 Besides the articles of buckskin that are produced in the interior, cotton blankets, sack cloth, and woolens are woven. I have seen coverlets that in their variety of design and beauty of color are much better [than others] in New Spain. . . If workers were provided the help they need, the unfavorable balance of trade would be corrected.

And is this so difficult? Hardly a day goes by that the [Mexican courts] do not sentence to prison for some small crime, Indians or common folk who are loom makers, weavers, fullers, dyers, embroiderers, hatters, etc. Some of them could be sent here, if the matter were handled properly. Outcasts could establish themselves to good advantage. . .if they minded their ways, and they would probably turn out to be very good settlers. 99

A missionary's letter to his superiors in 1778.

Every spring workers planted their crops, watched over the births of calves, colts, and lambs, repaired leaky ditches, and sheared the sheep of their wool grown over the winter. In the courtyard, if the weather was nice, the women gathered to card, wash, spin, and dye the wool. Men were usually the weavers who transformed the yarn into clothing, bed blankets, horse blankets, and rugs for the ranch as well as for barter when the caravan arrived.

In autumn the workers took scythes to the fields to cut the ripened wheat, which they carried to a small corral and spread on the ground. Horses, burros, goats, or sheep would be driven slowly around the pen, crushing and separating the kernels of grain from the stalks under their hooves. On a Spanish ranch, nothing went to waste. When the grain had been stored or ground into flour, the crushed stalks were used to stuff mattresses. Mature animals were butchered and eaten, or their meat smoked or salted for future use. The hides were

SARAPE Wool from sheep brought over by the Spanish, combined with Indian weaving, led to a textile industry in northern Mexico. *Sarapes*, or "wearing blankets," were especially prized by horsemen.

tanned and stored for trade, or cut and sewn into long-wearing clothes; steer horns were carved into blowing horns or fancy drinking cups. Fat went into cooking, and to make candles and soap; horsehair was woven into elegant hatbands, bridles, and rope; even leftover blood was mixed with meat to make tasty sausage.

Religious devotion was ingrained in the lives of everyone on the ranch. Family members, ranch hands, and servants stopped in the chapel daily to light a candle, kneel, and pray for the sick or the dead. The arrival of a traveling *padre* was a highlight of ranch life. The visiting priest would say Mass, hear confessions, perform a wedding, baptism, or funeral, and give everyone his blessing. Before departing, a favorite father might preside over an evening fiesta the family and ranch hands gave in his honor.

REBOZO
The very fine handwork in a New Mexican *rebozo*, or shawl, suggests that it was reserved for special occasions. The rows of dancing figures are thought to represent a wedding.

MISSIONS: NEW CITIES OF GOD

The Franciscan fathers who first came to California made the journey to save Indian souls.

In the 21 missions founded along the coast the groundwork was laid for the

region's farming and ranching cultures, while their converts struggled to conform to alien ways.

OF ALL THE ROYAL ROADS blazed by the Spanish in the Americas, the one stretching nearly 700 miles from San Diego to Sonoma best exemplified their attempts at *conquista espiritual,* or colonization by conversion. Though their explorers and soldiers continued to scour new territory for "cities of gold," the Spanish friars concentrated on building new cities of God.

Along California's El Camino Real during the late 18th and early 19th centuries there flourished a chain of 21 missions, strategically located about a day's travel, or 30 miles, apart. Begun under the leadership of Fray Junípero Serra, a dedicated Franciscan considered the founder of California, these outposts formed the basis of the great ranching economies—and gave their names to some cities —of today's Golden State.

From San Diego de Alcalá, which Serra established in 1769, northward through the wilderness toward what would become San Francisco, the missions were at first little more than huts made of poles plastered

PAINTING ON HIDE
Saint Francis of Assisi, founder of the order that established most of California's missions, gazes out from this painting on animal hide. Such pictures were used to instruct Indian converts.

with mud. But as the friars, offering food and trinkets, lured more and more local Indians to worship and work, the largest missions grew into self-sufficient fiefdoms. Crops and livestock sustained the inhabitants and provided hides and tallow to distant markets.

Life in the mission followed a strict routine. Indian converts were called to Mass every morning by the mission's bells. After worship, a *pozole,* or stew of beans and chili or meat, was served from huge pots. Then the day's work began.

Usually there were two friars in charge of the mission, an elder to administer religious education and business, and a younger one who supervised the ranch labor. The neophytes, as converts were called, worked in the vegetable gardens, grainfields, and vineyards, tended the olive and orange groves, rode as vaqueros to drive the mission's herds of long-horned cattle, or acted as shepherds for its flocks of sheep. Others operated the looms that wove the raw wool into blankets and rugs, tended the vats in which animal fat was reduced to tallow for candles or soap, or worked in the gristmill or pottery shop. At noon the church bells rang again to announce a

MISSION LIFE

Drawn by promises of food and safety as well as religious

teaching, Indians learned new skills under the padres.

IN CALIFORNIA, as in other Spanish territories, the most imposing part of a mission was its church, which was often crowned by a dome and bell tower, or by a *campanario*, a simple, freestanding wall with arched openings for bells. In California, disastrous earthquakes and fires (some set by the flaming arrows of Indian warriors) led the friars to replace their first rough structures with buildings of sturdy white-washed adobe, sometimes fortified with massive buttresses and roofed with the familiar red "mission" tile. Walls were built four feet thick, to support the weight of the heavy log roof beams and roofs.

The church was connected by an arched cloister, laid out in a rough quadrangle, to living quarters for the padres, bunkrooms for soldiers assigned to the mission, storerooms, and a central kitchen. Nearby were workshops in which the Indian mission dwellers were taught trades like carpentry, tanning, weaving, and spinning. Beyond the barrack-like dormitories for single Indian women and men were the corrals, blacksmith shop, vegetable gardens, grain fields, and pastures. Usually the nearest Indian village was not far away.

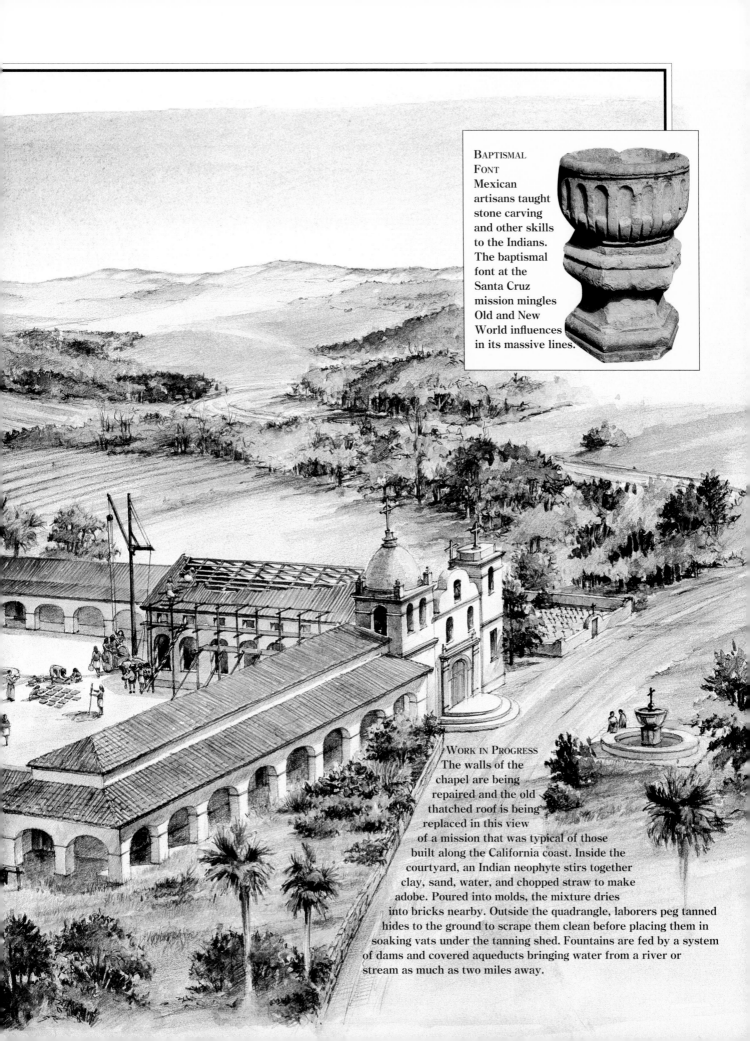

BAPTISMAL FONT Mexican artisans taught stone carving and other skills to the Indians. The baptismal font at the Santa Cruz mission mingles Old and New World influences in its massive lines.

WORK IN PROGRESS The walls of the chapel are being repaired and the old thatched roof is being replaced in this view of a mission that was typical of those built along the California coast. Inside the courtyard, an Indian neophyte stirs together clay, sand, water, and chopped straw to make adobe. Poured into molds, the mixture dries into bricks nearby. Outside the quadrangle, laborers peg tanned hides to the ground to scrape them clean before placing them in soaking vats under the tanning shed. Fountains are fed by a system of dams and covered aqueducts bringing water from a river or stream as much as two miles away.

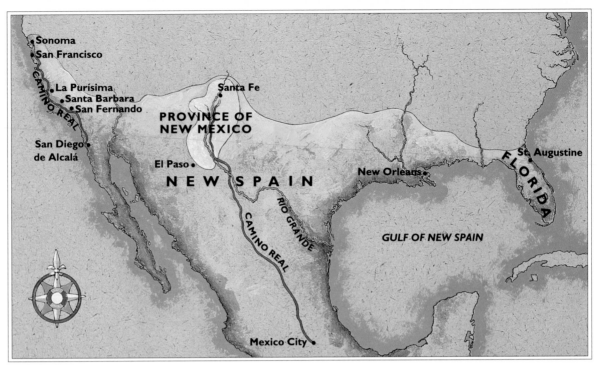

SPANISH LANDS   At the time of this map, about 1800, settlements of New Spain, shown in gold, stretched across North America's southern rim. Although the French founded New Orleans, King Louis XV had signed it over to Spain in 1763 and Spanish rule lasted there until 1803, when Louisiana became part of the United States.

midday meal of *atole,* or porridge. The evening meal varied only slightly from the previous two, though on holidays there might be a serving of foaming chocolate. Then there was time to tell stories, or make music with traditional Indian flutes, whistles, and rattles.

Only on Sundays did the routine vary. In the morning there was an even longer Mass, at which an Indian choir trained by the friars might perform sacred music. Afterwards, the men played native ball games.

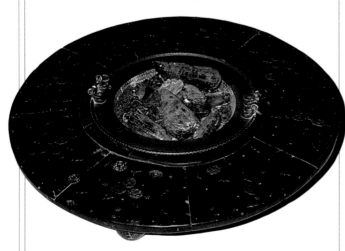

WARMING COALS   A charcoal brazier set in the center of the floor took the chill off a drafty room. Spanish braziers like this have been found from St. Augustine to the California mission at Carmel.

From the beginning, however, all was not well in the cities of God. Many Indians, used to freer ways, resented being beaten for minor transgressions and fled from the missions. Even worse were the periodic waves of European diseases—smallpox, mumps, measles—to which the Indians had no natural resistance, that swept through their ranks with devastating effects. At Mission La Purísima, north of Santa Barbara, disease, defections, and a dwindling supply of new converts reduced the Indian population from 1,520 in 1804 to less than 200 in four decades.

As one observer put it: "It must have caused many of the Fathers a severe pang to realize…that they were saving souls at the inevitable cost of lives. And yet such was the overwhelming fact. The brute upshot of colonization, in spite of its kindly flavor and humanitarian root, was only one thing—death."

After the independence of Mexico in 1821, the missions lost government support, and were officially secularized in 1834. The fate of both Indians and padres was sealed as religious influence shifted to parish churches and mission lands were gradually taken over by settlers from other parts of North America, drawn by the ceding of California to the United States in 1848. Ironically, gold—which had eluded the Spanish north of Mexico for two centuries—was discovered the very next day in a place called Sutter's Mill.

THE ENGLISH ARRIVE

MAP OF VIRGINIA BY JOHN WHITE

Landing initially at Jamestown and Plymouth, settlers from England

set the stage for two quite different ways of life. The adventurers of Virginia built

an economy based on the tobacco trade, laying the foundations

for the large slave-owning plantations of the South. Pious Puritans developed

New England's pattern of small farms and close-knit villages,

which were founded on self-government and strict adherence to the word of God.

ORDEAL AT JAMESTOWN

Virginia's early fortune-seekers found no gold or silver, no passage to the Orient,

only fiercely hostile tribesmen, starvation, and disease. They were ready to give up—until

John Rolfe discovered the profits that could be made from a "stinking weed."

IN THE WORDS OF Capt. John Smith, the red-bearded soldier of fortune who became Jamestown's most celebrated colonist: "There were never Englishmen left in a foreign country in such misery as we."

Indeed, the story of the first permanent English settlement in North America is one of frequent suffering, violence, sickness, and death. But by 1699, when Jamestown ceased to be a colonial capital, it had helped to establish England's claims to the continent. It had also left a legacy of devastating Indian warfare, the beginnings of the colonial tobacco and slave trades, and the lordly plantation economy that was to dominate life in the South.

The tale begins in May 1607, when three small ships carrying 104 men and boys arrived in Chesapeake Bay, lured by promises of easy wealth. Described as "adventurers" by their financial sponsor, the Virginia Company of London, they sailed some 50 miles up a broad river, marveling at "faire meddowes and goodly tall trees" on every side.

As a site for settlement, they picked a low-lying peninsula, well placed for defense and surrounded by water deep enough for docking. They christened both the river and their future "James Cittie" after their king, and began building a rough log fort.

Few who had made the voyage land were prepared for the rigorous work of carving a new town out of the wilderness. About half were carpenters, bricklayers, and laborers; the other half were "gentlemen," who

TRADE FOR FOOD The men of Jamestown brought copper and other European trade goods upriver to the villages of the Paspahegh Indians to barter for "victuals, as bread, corn, fish, and flesh in great plenty." When supplies in the colony ran low, however, John Smith used the threat of force to get corn from the Indians.

had been misled by rumors and published accounts about the New World, and expected to get rich by plucking pearls from oyster beds along the riverbank or digging for gold.

Laboring harder than many had ever worked before, in a climate far south of their native England, the men found their strength sapped by the unaccustomed heat. The choice of location also proved to be a mistake. Tidal flow made the peninsula's water supply brackish, and disease-spreading mosquitoes bred abundantly in the nearby swamps, causing many settlers to fall sick.

From the time the English landed, Indians had been watching them from the surrounding woods, and when the fort was about half completed the natives attacked, killing a boy and wounding 11 men before being driven off by cannon fire from the ships.

The frightened colonists hastened to complete the fort. They also built a crude church, and replaced their first makeshift tents with houses of "wattle and daub," like some of the poorest dwellings in England. These structures were made of saplings woven together and plastered over with mud and then roofed with thatch.

But few men were willing to plant and tend crops. Smith, the expedition's military expert, soon saw that the group was not even equipped to protect itself, much less produce an adequate supply of food. Smith organized the men into small bands, armed them with inaccurate but noisy muskets, and led forays upriver to Indian villages. Without a common language, the Europeans still managed to make the Indians under-

SMITH'S RESCUE An engraving from John Smith's *Generall Historie of Virginia* shows Pocahontas pleading with Powhatan to spare the Englishman's life. Pocahontas later married John Rolfe.

stand their desire to trade for food. At times Smith also made clear that if the supplies were not forthcoming, he would use the guns to claim them as "tribute."

On one trip, tribesmen captured Smith and took him before Powhatan, the most powerful chieftain in the region. According to Smith's account, Powhatan was about to have him put to death when the chief's 12-year-old daughter, Pocahontas, rushed forward to save him, cradling his head in her arms. Today, historians question whether this dramatic rescue actually

INSIDE THE PALISADE, LAWS FOR PRACTICAL LIVING

66There shall no man or woman, Launderer or Laundresse, dare wash any unclean Linen...or throw out the water or suds of fowle cloathes, in the open streete, within the Palizadoes.... Nor shall anyone aforesaid, within less than a quarter of one mile from the Palizadoes, dare to doe the necessities of nature, since by these unmanly, slothfull, and loathesome immodesties, the whole fort may bee choked, and poisoned

JAMESTOWN FORT Cannons were poised at each corner bastion.

with ill aires.... Every man shall have an especiall and due care, to keepe his house sweete and cleane, as also so much of the street as lieth before

his door, and...set his bedstead whereon he lieth, that it may stand three foote at least from the ground.... Every tradesman in there severall occupation...shall duly and daily attend his worke...upon perill for his first fault, to have his entertainment checkt for one month...and if he continue...to the galley for three yeare.99

Laws governing Jamestown in 1611.

A Legacy of the Lost Colony

I N 1587, 20 YEARS BEFORE the founding of Jamestown, a band of 150 English men, women, and children landed on Roanoke Island, off the coast of what is now North Carolina, planning eventually to move their settlement inland. One month later their governor, John White, persuaded of the need to procure more supplies, reluctantly sailed for England, taking paintings he had made of plants and animals and the friendly Secotan Indians who lived nearby. Among the settlers he left behind was his infant granddaughter, Virginia Dare, the first child born to European parents in America. Prolonged hostilities between England and Spain kept White from returning for three years, and when he finally reached the settlement it was abandoned. No survivors would ever be found; the only clue to their fate was the word Croatoan, the name of a nearby island, carved on a tree. Today White's paintings are the most lasting legacy of the lost colony at Roanoke, highly valued for the insights they provide into Indian life at the time Europeans began to arrive.

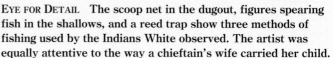

EYE FOR DETAIL   The scoop net in the dugout, figures spearing fish in the shallows, and a reed trap show three methods of fishing used by the Indians White observed. The artist was equally attentive to the way a chieftain's wife carried her child.

took place, since Smith wrote two versions of the Jamestown venture and failed to mention the incident until the second, which he published in 1624. If the event did occur, it may have helped the Indians and settlers reach the uneasy peace that allowed them to trade for the food the Europeans so badly needed.

Inside the fort, conditions were terrible during the colony's first winter. Many suffered from malaria, typhoid, and malnutrition. A fire swept through the thatched roofs and destroyed many houses, forcing the colonists to rebuild. This time they strengthened their fort with a high, triangular palisade.

In 1608, two ships arrived with more settlers, including the first women to reach the colony. But the newcomers proved no better suited than the first group to handle frontier life. Smith, promoted to commander of the settlement, wrote to England pleading with the colony's backers to send "carpenters, gardeners, fishermen, blacksmiths, masons" instead of the riffraff who had arrived so far and who threatened to consume the colony's resources "before they can be made good for anything."

In 1609 an injury caused by a gunpowder explosion forced Smith to return to England. The colony, without his strong leadership, reached its lowest ebb. After 30 settlers were massacred in an Indian village, the survivors retreated inside the fort, afraid to tend their fields, and the winter that followed would be remembered as "the starving time." Eating everything available—dogs, cats, mice, snakes, even their own shoes—many still died of malnutrition and disease. When new settlers arrived in May 1610, they found only 60 of some 500 colonists still alive.

THE GOLDEN WEED

The men at Jamestown tried starting trades—ironworking, glass-blowing, silk-making—to make the colony self-supporting. They cut and shipped walnut and cedar logs back to England and harvested sassafras root, popular for its medicinal properties; but none of these products gave the London investors an adequate profit.

Finally, the efforts of one colonist, John Rolfe, paid off. In Europe the use of tobacco was becoming popular. The Spanish grew it for export in the West Indies, and North American Indians also cultivated a harsh variety that they smoked in clay pipes. Rolfe's innovation was to obtain the sweeter West Indian seeds and improve the curing method. In 1614 Rolfe shipped his first four barrels of tobacco to England—and Jamestown had a money-making enterprise.

Tobacco was a demanding crop, requiring the planter's attention for most of the year. In late February or early March the seeds were planted in shallow wooden flats. As they sprouted, they were protected from frost with coverings of straw or brush, which were removed as the weather warmed to expose the seedlings to the sun. In early April the young plants were transferred to the fields, where they were set in the ground, one by one.

Through the summer, which could be swelteringly hot, the planter would have to prune his plants, keep them free of worms and pests, and hoe around them to remove the weeds. In August the stalks were cut and

TOBACCO LABEL
The three dominant figures in the Chesapeake tobacco culture—the Indian, the slave, and the planter—ornament this 18th-century tobacco label advertising a York River grower's crop.

the big leaves were hung to dry under open sheds. In October, when the leaves were properly cured, the planter stripped them from the stalks, chopped them, and pressed them into large barrels called hogsheads. Finally, in early December, when tobacco merchant ships arrived at the planter's dock, the hogsheads were rolled onto the wharf and hauled aboard.

Profits from tobacco made the hard work worth it. Settlers began to clear fields along every river around the Chesapeake Bay for the crop one observer called "that chopping herbe of Hell," and visitors to Jamestown found the plants growing in the streets. By 1619 the colony exported nearly 50,000 pounds of tobacco a year; by the late 1630's the amount had burgeoned to more than a million pounds.

Because tobacco quickly depleted the soil, farmers were continuously clearing new land. The crop also demanded intensive labor. To fill that need, indentured servants were imported to Virginia. In return for ocean passage, young men would agree to be legally bound for four years or more to work the fields of landowners, who supplied them with shelter, food, and clothing. When the term of servitude ended, the laborers each received 50 acres of land and a new set of clothes.

THE "CHOPPING HERBE OF HELL"

FROM THE TIME tobacco came into use in Europe, the benefits and drawbacks of the plant—sometimes called "sotweed"—were hotly debated. Early promoters touted it as a cure for everything from snakebite to hangovers.

One of the sternest opponents of tobacco smoking was England's King James I, who published *A Counter-blast to Tobacco* in 1604, in which he described the popular pastime as "a custome loathsome to the eye, hateful to the nose, harmfull to the brains, dangerous to the lungs, and in the blacke stinking fume thereof, neerest resembling the horrible Stigian smoke of the pit that is bottomlesse."

His eloquence notwithstanding, the king was also the royal sponsor for the establishment of Virginia, the colony described by Thomas Jefferson more than a century later as "founded on smoke."

SOCIABLE SMOKE
An 18th-century cartoon depicts smokers enjoying their pipes in a tavern. The botanical engraving shows the variety that John Rolfe developed.

Women also came to the colonies under terms of indenture, usually as house servants. In the early years, however, they came in far fewer numbers than the men. Unlike the Spanish, the English rarely married native women, and so for a long time the growth of the colony was limited. To improve the situation, the London Company sponsored the arrival, in 1620, of 90 young women touted as "pure and spotless." They were so welcome that each fetched the company the handsome price, in what had become the colony's main currency, of 120 pounds of tobacco.

That same year 20 blacks brought from the West Indies on a Dutch ship became the first of their race to reach the colony. Employed as laborers in the tobacco fields, they had status similar to white indentured servants in the early years. Slavery did not start to become an entrenched part of the plantation culture until the late 1600's.

As the colony gradually took root and prospered, its people also began to want more of a say in their own affairs. In 1619 the London company met their demands by authorizing the formation of a House of Burgesses. When its 31 members, all leading planters, met for the first time in the Jamestown fort, the town had grown well beyond its walls. In place of the old dwellings of wattle and daub were substantial houses of clapboard, two stories high. But access to the peninsula was guarded by a blockhouse, and dangers to the town had not ended. In 1622 pent-up Indian resentments erupted in raids on the plantations that claimed the lives of 347 settlers; then an epidemic followed, killing twice that many. Overall, in the first two decades after the founding of Jamestown, some 6,000 out of the original 7,000 settlers perished.

After mismanagement eventually caused the London company's charter to be revoked, the town became the seat of the new royal colony of Virginia. In 1699 the capital was moved to higher ground, between the York and the James Rivers, a site called Middle Plantation. Within a year the name of the new government seat, destined to grow into a brilliant and beautiful town, had been changed to Williamsburg.

PRECIOUS CARGO Barrels of tobacco are rolled aboard a London-bound ship as Jamestown's tobacco boom begins. In 1618, only a half-dozen years after the settlers began to grow the crop, Jamestown sent 50,000 pounds of dried tobacco to England. By the middle of the 17th century tobacco growers were all packing the leaves into barrels of a standard size, nearly four feet high and weighing about 475 pounds when filled.

PILGRIM DAYS AT PLYMOUTH

New England's first colonists struggled to cope with a harsh and unfamiliar

land while they established their village at a site named by King Charles I. They survived with

the help of friendly Indians, with whom they celebrated a memorable Thanksgiving.

WHEN THE MAYFLOWER dropped anchor off the New England coast late in 1620, the leading passengers among the 102 souls aboard were quite different from the Jamestown group that had preceded them to the new land. England's second lasting colony in the New World included mature married men, their wives and children— and in a few cases, the families' indentured servants.

Moreover, they had not crossed the ocean in search of wealth; what some of the voyagers sought was the freedom to worship as they pleased. They were Protestant dissenters known in England as "Separatists" because they had refused to follow the practices of the Church of England, which they considered too similar to those of the Catholic Church. None of the group called themselves pilgrims—that name came 10 years later, when Governor William Bradford wrote, referring to a biblical passage to describe the colony's founding days, "they knew they were pilgrimes." The term did not gain widespread use until about 1800.

As founders of a colony, the settlers called themselves planters. Along with the strongly religious-minded among them were seamen, craftsmen, and laborers recruited by the London investors who co-sponsored the venture. All were hardworking people, and most dressed in the rough, sturdy garb of English yeomen. The men wore breeches and doublets of canvas

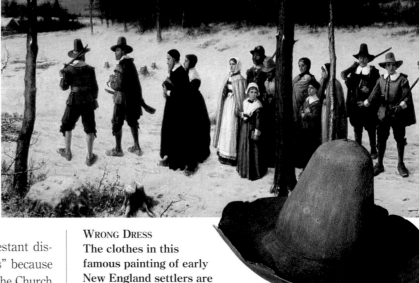

WRONG DRESS
The clothes in this famous painting of early New England settlers are wrong in most details except for the men's hats, a style worn in Europe by men and women in the 17th century. The hat at right belonged to a member of the founding colony at Plymouth.

or wool, and the clothing of the women was often richly colored, in shades of violet, red, or blue, set off by an apron and a hat or close-fitting cap.

Delayed by troubles in departure and errors in navigation, the *Mayflower* voyagers did not reach their destination until November, when winter had already set in. While most of the passengers remained in their cramped and stuffy quarters on board the ship, some went ashore in scouting parties to choose a site for settlement. When a hillside location overlooking the shore was decided on, the colonists began building their settlement on Christmas day, felling trees for a "common house" for storing their rapidly dwindling supplies. The work was no violation of the beliefs of the religious group, since its members considered the observance of Christmas "popish."

WICKER CRADLE
The first child born to the Plymouth colonists, Peregrine White, slept in this cradle on board the *Mayflower*.

The name Plymouth had been chosen for the site in 1614 by King Charles I, then Prince Charles, for a map made by John Smith. It was also the name of the last English port from which the *Mayflower* sailed, but that winter the port of arrival was no safe haven. More than half the inhabitants, weak from the arduous voyage, during which they had subsisted on a prolonged diet that included little except biscuits and salt beef, died from malnutrition, exposure, and disease.

In March of 1621 the last of the *Mayflower* voyagers were finally living ashore when the settlers were surprised by a visitor. An Indian named Samoset approached a group of the colonists and asked in English for beer. Samoset later revisited the colony with a friend, Squanto, who was a Wampanoag Indian and the last surviving member of the community that had formerly occupied the Plymouth site. The European fishermen and fur traders who had plied the New England coast

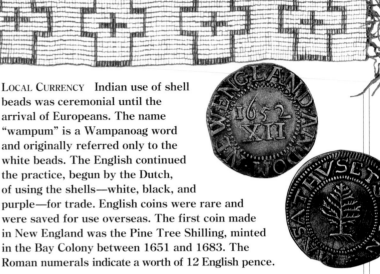

LOCAL CURRENCY Indian use of shell beads was ceremonial until the arrival of Europeans. The name "wampum" is a Wampanoag word and originally referred only to the white beads. The English continued the practice, begun by the Dutch, of using the shells—white, black, and purple—for trade. English coins were rare and were saved for use overseas. The first coin made in New England was the Pine Tree Shilling, minted in the Bay Colony between 1651 and 1683. The Roman numerals indicate a worth of 12 English pence.

and introduced the Indians to beer had also brought the disease, probably smallpox, that decimated the Wampanoag tribe.

Squanto was even more familiar than Samoset with English ways. Some years earlier he had been captured by slave-trading fishermen and spent time in England. To these pious folk at Plymouth, barely clinging to survival, the tribesman appeared as a veritable gift from God. He taught them how to hunt and fish; he pointed out which local berries and nuts were edible; he showed them the right way to plant native corn, pumpkins, and beans, and how to fertilize their crops by planting seeds with herring, which spawned in nearby streams each spring.

REASON FOR CELEBRATION

In the fall of 1621, Plymouth's residents were able to gather a harvest bountiful enough to allow a joyful feast. Indian corn and meal, along with cod and other dried fish, had been stored in portions sufficient to supply all the colonists through the upcoming winter. Nuts and berries were as plentiful as the ripened crops from the gardens and fields, and hunters had brought in ducks, geese, venison, and "a great store of wild turkeys." The great Wampanoag chieftain, Massasoit, attended the gathering, arriving with 90 braves. The Indians brought five fresh-killed deer, the hosts entertained their guests by demonstrating the firing power of their muskets, and the celebration lasted three days. Today the holiday observance of Thanksgiving still commemorates that time of recovery and hope.

CHRISTMAS CARTOON A 1653 broadside shows an English Puritan turning away Father Christmas. The print was published to mock the Puritans' scornful attitude toward the holiday.

By the spring of 1622, when 60 more settlers arrived, Plymouth Plantation was a village with two rows of thatch-roofed houses ascending a hill inside a new wooden palisade. That summer, after news of the Indian massacre at Jamestown reached the colony, the settlers built a fort on the hill inside the town walls, and posted a watch on the wooden ramparts where cannon stood ready to fire. The New England settlers were careful to maintain good relations with the nearby natives, but they did not leave their security to chance. There was never a need to fire the cannon in defense of Plymouth, however, and the room downstairs in the fort was used for meetings and religious services.

To pay their debt to the investors who had underwritten their voyage, the Plymouth settlers cut oak trees into clapboard and pipestaves they sent to England, and they established trade with the Indians in beaver pelts and other furs of the region. In 1604 the quality of life in the colony improved after a ship arrived with the first cattle the settlers had seen since departing from England. In 1625 Governor Bradford wrote that the people "never felt the sweetness of the country until this year." It was not until 1648, however, that the colony was entirely free of debt to its backers. By that time the inhabitants of Plymouth had many English neighbors.

PROVISIONS LIST

4 peares of shoes

4 peares of stockings

1 peare Norwich gaiters

4 shirts

2 suits dublet and hose of leather, ye hose & dublett with hooks & eyes

1 suit of Nordon dussens or hampshire kersies lyn'd the hose with skins, dublets with lynen of gilford or gedlyman kerseys

4 bands

2 handkerchiefs

1 wastecoat of greene cotton bound about with red tape

1 leather girdle

1 Monmouth cap

1 black hatt lyned in the brows with leather

5 Red Knitt capps mill'd about 5d. apiece

2 peares of gloves

1 Mandillion [mantle or great coat] lyned with cotton

1 peare of breaches and waistcoat

1 leather sute of Dublett & breeches of oyled leather

CUTTING CLAPBOARDS   A wooden mallet and an iron-bladed frow were the tools used to "rive" boards out of logs in four-foot lengths.

SURVIVAL GEAR   After stories of Plymouth's early days reached England, lists were published recommending how New England settlers should equip themselves. Above are men's clothes considered necessary in the colonies in 1629.

A CARGO OF COWS

Plymouth, a village of about 20 simple houses,

saw its quality of life transformed by a quartet of cattle.

IN MARCH 1624 the English ship *Charity* reached Plymouth with a welcome cargo of fresh supplies that included a bull and three cows—the first cattle seen by the colonists since they had set sail from their homeland more

than three years before. Chickens, pigs, and goats were raised in the settlement (the only animals known to have made the voyage aboard the *Mayflower* were two dogs), so goats' milk and cheese were available, but the opportunity to

have fresh cow's milk, butter, and cheese meant an immediate improvement in the community's standard of living. The settlers could also foresee the herd that could grow from this stock and eventually supply fresh meat, hides for clothing and shoes, and the tallow necessary for making candles, a luxury generally too expensive for the colonists to import.

The animals were small compared to breeds known today. One was red, two were black, and the bull, of unknown general color, had a white stripe on

its back. At the time of their arrival, Plymouth was a village of about 20 single-room cottages facing each other along a single street. Roofs were shingle or thatch and built at a steep pitch to shed both rain and snow. Luxuriant forests nearby guaranteed the colonist an ample supply of wood. In England by the 1600's the forests had been greatly reduced by the needs of its fast-growing population for building materials and firewood. The colonists' houses were built on upright frames of oak studs, covered with wattle and daub; clapboard was added for protection against the elements. Since rock was scarce, chimneys were also wattle and daub, and in constant danger of catching fire.

RUSH LAMP
The dried reed held in this clamp was soaked in grease, and was smelly and smokey while it burned. Most lamps of the time were equally disagreeable.

THE PURITAN HOME AND HEARTH

The lives of Puritan families centered on small, snug houses in which a single

room with a huge fireplace served for cooking, eating, sleeping, and most other activities.

Meals, eaten with fingers or wooden spoons, were chiefly based on corn.

BY THE LATE 1620's, when Plymouth settlers were moving north to set up outposts for fur trading, more English immigrants were beginning to arrive along the New England coast. In 1630, 1,000 people, led by John Winthrop, governor of the new Massachusetts Bay Colony, landed in the area that would become Boston. By the early 1640's another 20,000 settlers had followed them.

Like the people of Plymouth, the newcomers around Massachusetts Bay sought a purer, simpler approach to worship than the Church of England permitted. Calling themselves Puritans, they tended to come from more prosperous backgrounds than the Plymouth set-

tlers; many were craftsmen or merchants, able to provide the new colonies with needed goods. Thanks to the Plymouth experience, moreover, they reached the New World better equipped, with adequate clothing and food supplies and proper tools.

On their arrival, the colonists improvised homes as best they could, living in tents, "English wigwams," sod-roofed dugouts, and even caves. As they were able, and with the help of their neighbors, the colonists built simple frame houses covered with rough-sawn boards and roofed with thatched grasses or reeds. But thatch easily caught fire, as did the houses' clay-lined wooden chimneys, and both were eventually outlawed.

ENGLISH WIGWAMS A 1630 account describes the homes of Indians near Salem as "made with small poles prik't into the ground...matted with boughs and covered with sedge and old mats." Colonists adapted the "wigwam" construction to their own use by adding a fireplace and door. Windows were small and covered with oiled paper, which allowed light into the room but provided no view.

Unfortunately, the brick chimneys that replaced them were not much safer, since constant use caused them to build up a coating of flammable soot. To clean the inside walls they couldn't reach with a broom, homeowners sometimes dropped one or two chickens down the chimney. The wild flapping of wings would knock the soot loose, while the bird's squawking descent provided the household with a little amusement.

By the late 1600's a typical Puritan home was a modest but sturdy dwelling, built around a central chimney, with one or more fireplaces to heat adjoining rooms. Better-built houses had an additional layer of clapboards to make them weather-tight, and some had casement windows imported from England with diamond-shaped panes of glass, which gradually replaced the oiled-paper window coverings that early settlers had used. Wooden latches, inside and out, were eventually replaced by latches made by the local blacksmith.

Interior walls were often plastered and whitewashed, but the house exteriors rarely saw paint, a costly commodity that was not generally available. When paint came into use in the 1700's, it was mostly a dark "Indian red" made of a local red earth mixed with fish oil, not the pristine white we associate with later New England towns.

LIFE IN THE HALL

In a Puritan home the focus of activity was the main room on the ground floor, called the "hall." Here meals were cooked in a cavernous fireplace up to 10 feet wide, with an iron crossbar to hold hanging pots and

kettles that were used for soap-boiling and candle-dipping as well as for preparing food. A brick oven for baking was built into the chimney, and often there was a built-in seat where the cook could warm herself while tending a stew. Members of the family would bathe in this room near the hearth, using water carried indoors in buckets from the well and heated over the fire.

Since it was used for almost everything,

EATING UTENSILS It was not until the 1700's that forks were used to carry food to the mouth; these two-tined forks served only to hold down meat for cutting. As life in the colonies improved, dishes of pewter replaced the lipped wooden plates known as trenchers.

TABLETOP RUG The first carpets in the colonies were used as coverings for tables rather than floors. Housewives followed the English practice of spreading rushes on the floor.

CHAIR MAN

In a Puritan home the table where the family ate was called "the board." The head of the household was sometimes referred to as the "chair man," since the use of that rare article of furniture was reserved for him. From such homely beginnings comes our powerful, resonant phrase, "chairman of the board."

EARLY NEW ENGLAND SCHOOLING

IN 1647, THE BAY COLONY'S government called on towns with more than 50 families to hire a schoolmaster "to teach all such children as resort to him to write and read." Most teachers were men, although some women ran "dame schools" for very young children. Schools were usually one-room affairs, where students of varying ages recited their lessons out loud. Paper was scarce, and early school texts consisted of a single sheet, bearing the alphabet, the Lord's Prayer, and a few common syllables. The paper was attached to a wooden paddle and protected by a thin covering of yellowish, transparent horn. In the 1700's, these hornbooks were replaced with early versions of the *New England Primer*. Students were encouraged to learn with rhymes like the following:

He who ne'er learns his ABC
Forever will a blockhead be
But he who learns his letters fair
Shall have a coach to take the air.

HORNBOOK Children sometimes hung these one-page "books" on string around their necks.

THE GOOD BOOK
In New England the high value placed on education was rooted in the importance of being able to read the Bible.

1670 PORTRAIT The painting of a beribboned New England boy proclaims the status some families enjoyed by the time it was executed. Fancy trim was reserved for the use of families of "gentlemen."

the hall was a busy place, cluttered with washtubs, barrels of staple goods, a spinning wheel, a hand loom for weaving cloth, and a churn for making butter and cheese. Smoked slabs of bacon, strings of dried apples, and ears of corn saved for seed hung from the ceiling beams. A chest or two for bedding and clothes stood against a wall. If the hall was also the bedroom of the husband and wife, they might sleep on a "jack" bed, built into a corner so that it was joined to the walls on two sides, requiring a single corner post for support. Under the bed there was frequently a trundle bed, pulled out at night, where the young children of the family could sleep.

In early colonial households meals were often eaten at a table that consisted of a wide, rough-hewn plank that rested on trestles and was referred to as "the board," leading to the expression "bed and board." Chairs were scarce, though the hall might have a rough stool or two. In the absence of seating, family members, especially children, would eat standing up. They ladled their food from a common pot, and several might share a serving on a flat wooden plate with a lipped edge, called a trencher. They ate with their fingers, or with knives or wooden spoons, since forks were still rarities. For a while the only fork in

Massachusetts was reputed to belong to Governor Winthrop, who had brought it from England on the ship *Arbella,* tucked in its own carrying case.

Beverages like beer, cider, or milk were drunk from a tankard or jug, passed around and shared on demand. (One Puritan child interrupted a guest who had placed his lips hesitantly on the rim with the warning, "You're using Grandma's place!") Earthenware and pewter were common; costly china and silver were not. The will of Lionel Chute, an Ipswich schoolteacher, suggests how treasured an heirloom an item of silver could be. When Chute died, in 1645, he bequeathed the one piece of silver he owned—his spoon—to his son James.

Boiled meats, vegetables, and stews were relished by the colonists, but much of the time they lived on native corn, which the Indians called maize. Corn bread was a daily staple, as was cornmeal mush, known as "hasty pudding." A tastier dish was "Indian pudding," corn meal boiled with molasses in a bag. From the Indians the colonists learned to make a winter delicacy called *misickquatash,* or "succotash," which included corn and kidney beans cooked in bear grease. After corn was eaten, the cobs were saved to make pipe bowls, jug stoppers, and children's dolls. Mattresses were stuffed with the husks, and the stalks were used for livestock fodder.

In the early years, before barley was a widely grown crop in the colonies, the settlers roasted young corn and fermented it with yeast to make a low-alcohol brew. By the 1650's beer was often consumed, even by children, at meals, and cider was equally common. By the late 1600's rum had become popular— too popular, some ministers thought. If the household could afford it, a bottle of Madeira wine was kept for serving on special occasions. The early colonists seem to have had an aversion to drinking plain water, distrusting its origins and potential effects on their health.

Below the main room in most homes was a cellar for storage and supplies of winter food; above was a loft, which provided space for more storage and for older children to stretch out on bedrolls at night.

As families prospered they would improve their houses by building new rooms, usually in the form of a lean-to, or "linter," across the back of the house. The new area would include a kitchen and a smaller private room for the husband and wife. On the outside of the house the addition gave rise to the familiar New England saltbox shape. Inside, the former hall became the parlor, or "best room," for entertaining guests. If a family grew truly prosperous, the walls might be covered in "painted paper" imported from England.

Kitchen Garden Remedies

Just beyond the doorway leading from every New England kitchen lay the housewife's kitchen garden, where the seeds of favorite English root vegetables—turnips, carrots, onions—flourished in New World soil. Since few medically trained men came to early New England, the housewife was relied upon to grow medicinal herbs and prepare remedies to alleviate her family's ills.

Books from England were a popular source of the recipes she would use for the syrups, oils, and distillations believed to heal. *The Queen's Closet Opened,* published in 1655, offered "incomparable secrets in Physick, Chyrurgery, Preserving, Candying & Cookery" including the protective "perfume" below. John Josselyn visited his brother in Maine and wrote *New England Rarities Discovered,* which offered the unlikely eyewash. Given medical knowledge at the time, such brews would not have been very different from a physician's.

Perfume Against the Plague

Take Angelica roots, and dry them a very little in an Oven, or by the fire; and then bruise them very soft, and lay them in Wine Vinegar to steep, being close covered three or four days, and then heat a brick hot, and lay the same thereon every morning; this is excellent to air the house or any clothes, or to breathe over in the morning fasting.

An Excellent Water For Ye Sight

Take Sage, Fennel, Vervain, Bettony, Eyebright, Celandine, Cinquefoyle, Herb of Grass, pimpernel. Steep them in white wine one night, distil them altogether, and use the water to wash the Eyes.

GOD-FEARING COMMUNITIES

In New England villages, citizens were bound together by common origins

and convictions, but reactions to outsiders could be rigid. Eventually some Puritan views had

to yield either to the emergence of new leadership or the founding of new colonies.

AS FAMILY LIFE in colonial New England centered on the home and hearth, community life revolved around the village with its centrally used land and its meeting house.

When a group of families, perhaps 50 or more, had chosen a suitable site for a new town, with the colony's approval, farm land and house lots were parceled out around a central common, where the families pastured their livestock and built a simple meeting house to serve the community as both town hall and church. In laying out the village, social standing was strictly observed. The minister and other leaders in the community chose their plots of land first; those of lesser reputation drew lots for what remained. Land was also set aside for the community's burial ground.

At periodic town meetings, residents debated issues both large and small, from the education of the town's children down to whose cow had wandered into whose vegetable patch and what should be done. Attendance was compulsory, under penalty of fine.

A typical town, like Hadley, Massachusetts, was very much community-run. Everyone's livestock was herded together from the town common to the pastures and back at night. Rather than having a mayor to oversee municipal affairs, five part-time "selectmen" were chosen by their fellow citizens, who had to be male, property owners, and church members in order to vote. A host of less prestigious officials, paid "by the piece"

THE PURITANS AND WITCHCRAFT IN SALEM

IN THE SPRING OF 1692 a girl in the village of Salem, Massachusetts, became suddenly ill, experiencing convulsions and pains throughout her body. A washerwoman with whom the girl had argued was blamed, promptly arrested, tried, and convicted of being a witch.

Belief in witches as servants of the devil was commonplace in the 17th century, and was not considered in conflict with Puritan religious views. In Salem, however, Puritan zeal became allied with a hysterical fear of witches that permeated the village in 1692 and resulted in the executions of 14 women, 6 men, and even 2 dogs. Some historians believe that

the witch hunt ended because accusations began to spread into the upper levels of Salem society.

Although it lasted only four months, Salem's witch hunt reflected attitudes of Puritan intolerance at its worst. When the special "witch" court that had been convened was dissolved, 150 people who had been imprisoned were released and charges against almost 200 others were quietly dropped.

SALEM TRIAL Exaggerated gestures in a 19th-century painting suggest the hysteria that gripped the community.

HOURGLASS HOLDER
This beautifully wrought iron stand held an hourglass in the Woodstock, Connecticut, meeting house; it was placed to the right of the pulpit in view of the congregation. The glass might be turned four times before the preacher finished his sermon.

for the work they performed, included three assessors of property values; two constables, who doubled as policemen and tax collectors, and who carried long black staffs tipped with brass; four tithing men, who kept an eye on churchgoers as well as "Sabbath breakers, liquor sellers, tipplers, and nightwalkers"; two measurers of land, a gauger of casks, a hog ringer, a cow keeper, a shepherd, a gravedigger, and an armed Sabbath guard who acted as a sentinel while residents were in church. Every property owner was required to contribute one day of labor each year to the maintenance of the roads of the town, and another day for each acre of pasture he owned.

A DAY IN CHURCH

Each Sunday morning, the meeting house doubled as the scene of Congregationalist services, which were also compulsory. Parishioners were seated according to sex and social rank, the men on one side of the central aisle, the women and girls on the other. To forestall any nonsense, boys were sometimes placed up near the chancel under the minister's eye. Town officials and other prominent citizens were assigned pews nearest the front, followed by farmers and artisans, with common laborers and indentured servants sitting in back.

Sermons were prodigious, going on for two hours or more and invariably dealing with the wages of sin. After the morning service, there was time to socialize and go home for lunch. Then everyone trooped back to the meeting house for an afternoon service much like the morning's. Away from the church, decorum was also supposed to be observed. People who "broke the Sabbath" by doing housework, shaving, running, or kissing were subject to fines. Since it was generally believed that a child was born on the same day of the week that it was conceived, a couple might be fined if the wife gave birth on Sunday.

ATTENTION ON GOD
In a New England meeting house the prominent pulpit and wooden pews were built plain so that the congregation would not be distracted from the preaching of God's word.

FOOTWARMER AND TITHING STICK
If a listener dozed off, the tithing man, who also collected offerings, rapped the sleeper on the head. In winter, unless members of a congregation had brought their own foot stoves to the unheated hall, they usually endured the service wide-eyed and shivering.

The God-fearing Puritans, who lived strictly by the Bible, had severe laws to enforce their code. Drunkenness, vagrancy, petty thievery, and the wearing of excessive finery were punished by whipping, or by locking a culprit by the hands, head, or legs in wooden pillories or stocks located on the common for everyone to see. Serious crimes—adultery, rape, murder, treason, witchcraft—merited death by hanging, a major public spectacle in which the condemned was taken by cart to the gallows while villagers looked on.

Although residents of New England communities were markedly close-knit and neighborly among themselves, they could be as markedly unfriendly to anyone they had even the slightest reason to distrust. A stranger walking down the street was an immediate object of suspicion: What is he doing here? Is he a criminal, a vagrant, or a poor person for whom the town might have to become responsible? Is he the bearer of some disease? Unless a respectable citizen could vouch for him, the traveler was quickly "warned out" by a constable; if he persisted in lingering, he might be whipped.

The rigidity of Puritan life, however, was not to everyone's liking. People of independent mind often ignored or flouted laws they considered overly authoritarian. When the citizens of a town became divided over a local issue one group, led by a few prominent citizens, sometimes departed with like-minded neighbors to create a new town. In 1636 Thomas Hooker, a Congregationalist minister, led members of his flock from Newtowne (now Cambridge), Massachusetts, to Connecticut, where they joined in the founding of Hartford. That same year a fiery Welsh clergyman named Roger Williams, banished from Massachusetts for his practice of "soul liberty," moved south to found Providence, later the capital of Rhode Island, whose policies of religious toleration would have an impact on life far beyond its own borders.

NORTH AND SOUTH By 1700 the extent of English settlements, shown in red, reached well inland, but patterns of development differed sharply to the north and south. In New England, farmers rarely lived far from town, and social ties were strong. In the Chesapeake region, plantation culture was spread out and discouraged close communities.

FRONTIERS OF A NEW FRANCE

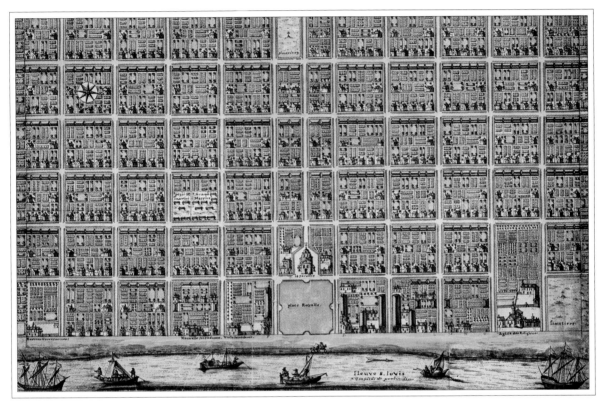

1755 CITY PLAN OF NEW ORLEANS

Drawn to North America by the promise of riches in the fur trade, Frenchmen

pushed deep into the northern wilderness, where many became

legendary as buckskin-clad traders and black-robed priests. French Protestants—

the Huguenots—settled throughout the English colonies and were welcomed

for their industry and skills. French explorers also ventured south

along the Mississippi River and planted a colony unique in its social mosaic,

its enthusiasm for celebrations, and, not least, its foods.

"Runners of the Woods"

When Europe developed a passion for New World furs, rugged young

Frenchmen fanned out across the Great Lakes region and adopted Indian ways. Outlawed for trading

without licenses, the men scarcely noticed as they pressed still deeper into the woods.

A CENTURY BEFORE the English landed at Jamestown, enterprising fishermen were crossing the North Atlantic from France to net bounteous catches of cod along the Grand Banks off the island of Newfoundland, near the mouth of the St. Lawrence River, and occasionally to barter for food and animal skins with natives on shore. In 1534 the explorer Jacques Cartier, seeking a passage to the Orient, sailed inland along the St. Lawrence. There he was surprised to find Indians who were familiar with simple trade goods like steel knives and iron pots—in exchange for which they eagerly offered stacks of luxurious pelts. In Europe the quality of New World furs

soon created a huge demand for the skins of muskrat, ermine, otter, and other animals, but above all for beaver. The animal's soft, barbed hairs could be made into a long-lasting felt used across Europe for high-crowned hats. By the 17th century hundreds of hardy young Frenchmen had sailed to the Canadian wilderness and established themselves in the fur trade, paddling birchbark canoes along the St. Lawrence and into the forested streams around the Great Lakes.

Along with the fur traders came equally hardy missionaries, mostly Jesuit priests, inspired by the vast number of souls in the New World not yet introduced to Christianity. Wearing the black cassocks that

Breaking Camp
Shortly past dawn, canoemen prepare to set off for their next trading site. One trapper brings in pelts from animals trapped overnight while others repack the canoe. A trader leaving to travel overland is assisted in loading his pack. The "tump-line" across his forehead eases the strain on his back.

earned them the Indians' nickname Black Robes, these men shared the same hardships and dangers, and often the paddling of the canoes, along river routes to the villages of Indian tribes living deep in the northern forests. Most of the early traders, called *coureurs de bois* ("runners of the woods"), were officially regarded as outlaws by the governors who had been sent to establish colonial rule in New France. When the government withheld the licenses for trading, the response of the coureurs was clear: they could not have cared less.

ON THE WATER

Dressed in buckskins and moccasins adopted from their Indian counterparts, their outfits set off by jaunty sashes and plumed caps, these vigorous vagabonds set out each spring from Montreal and other posts, squatting amid bales of trading supplies and equipment in their canoes. They paddled furiously from dawn until dusk,

FISH FORTUNES The codfish industry off Newfoundland grew into a thriving enterprise, as suggested in this 1705 illustration. Letters indicate steps in catching, cleaning, and drying the cod. The fisherman's fur garb attests to the abundance of pelts.

covering 60 to 80 miles a day. Along the way they would sing French folk songs and stop now and then for a pipe's worth of tobacco and a rest, during which a raconteur in the party might spin them a yarn. If the words of a song or story turned bawdy, as they usually did, the storyteller might get a disapproving (but unenforceable) glare from a priest hitching a ride to the frontier.

On the upstream voyage, the canoemen would have to wade in icy water up to their waists to tow their craft through an area of rapids. If this proved impossible, they unloaded and carried both canoes and cargoes on their backs, an arduous overland maneuver called a portage. Going downstream, they took pleasure in running rapids that posed a challenge to their manly skills; small white crosses along the riverbanks marked the many spots where some of the men paid for that bravado with their lives.

On the long journeys into the wilderness, the coureurs lived on two meals a day, both consisting of a ration of cornmeal mush fortified with salt pork, jerked venison, or dried fish, washed down with water from the cold stream. After the evening meal—and a nip of brandy to "aid the digestion"—most were happy to throw themselves on the ground by the fire, swat away flies, and sleep off their exhaustion until dawn. At the end of an unlucky day the men might have to spend several hours patching their canoes.

WILDERNESS CORPORATION The North West Company, situated on Lake Superior near the Canadian border, became the largest and most profitable trading post for hundreds of miles around in the late 1700's. Today the stockade, fur depot, and other buildings have been reconstructed at Grand Portage National Monument.

The speedy, lightweight crafts were fast and flexible, but the skins of birchbark were vulnerable in shallow, fast-moving water to puncture by rocks. To repair a hole, the men would apply a patch of birchbark and seal it in place with waterproofing pitch.

When they arrived at a trading post—generally a few log huts surrounded by a wooden palisade—the canoemen unpacked their goods. Knives, axes, kettles, blankets, and trinkets were the early items of trade; increasingly, though, their Indian customers wanted brandy, ammunition, and guns. July was the month when the Indians would gather in camps just outside the trading posts, ready to trade the precious pelts they had brought from farther inland. After a day spent haggling and swapping, the Frenchmen would have time to relax, drink, play cards, and perhaps seek the company of an Indian maid.

At the end of the trading season some canoemen would pack up their haul of furs and make the return voyage to Montreal, capital of the Great Lakes fur trade, or some other post from which they had started, before the rivers froze over for the winter. Others, without families to return to, moved deeper into the wilderness, visiting Indian villages, where they made connections that could increase the next season's trade. They might winter in one of those native vil-

lages or at a major post like Fort Chicago or Fort Detroit. Beyond the frontier, some settled down with Indian wives. Others, alone in the wilderness, simply disappeared, victims of accident, snakebite, disease, or Indian attack.

In the 1700's the ways of the coureurs were inherited by their successors, the *voyageurs* ("travelers"), men who were employed by the large French, Scottish, and English companies that had become dominant in the fur trade. These traders paddled huge canoes, 35 feet long, with crews of 12 men. In pursuit of fur harvests they pushed ever farther west, north, and south, building up rivalries among themselves and their companies for a share of the wealth.

It was a life that sometimes appalled but always impressed less adventurous souls, who marveled at the brawny physiques of the canoemen, their careless debauchery, their audacity, and their willingness to live for years at a time among the native tribes. Often the hard conditions of the work forced them out, still young, their bodies crippled by physical abuse and their dreams of wealth unrealized. The profits many might have amassed were spent on alcohol or gambled away. Yet it was a life of undeniable rewards. One retired voyageur summed it up: "Were I young again, I should glory in commencing the same career."

THE GIFTED HUGUENOTS

Protestants forced to flee persecution in France brought skills to the colonies

that made them welcome nearly everywhere they settled. Most were quickly assimilated

into their new communities, and many became prominent members of society.

OF ALL THE FRENCH pioneers, one group stood apart for the influence it exerted, out of proportion to its numbers, on early American life—not in the French colonies but in the predominantly English ones along the eastern seaboard. The Huguenots were French Protestants who left their native country for religious reasons, and by their industry and versatility turned exile into opportunity in the New World.

The first Huguenots to attempt settlement arrived off the southeastern coast in 1562, in three ships under the command of Jean Ribaut. They sailed along what is now Florida and Georgia until they landed on a coastal island in South Carolina, where they built a small post they called Charlesfort. Starvation and dissension eventually forced the settlers to give up, however, and most of the survivors returned to France.

It was not until a century later that more Huguenots began to arrive, prompted by an edict issued by Louis XIV in 1685 that made them subject to persecution as Protestants in a Catholic France. Many were skilled craftsmen—carpenters, blacksmiths, silversmiths, goldsmiths, weavers, wigmakers, shipwrights—whose services were welcomed in the growing English settlements, where most settlers were also Protestants.

GOLD RING
Simeon Soumaine, one of the few Huguenot goldsmiths known by name, was the maker of this delicately inscribed wedding band.

A number of Huguenot families, migrating from the same home villages, banded together to attempt new French-speaking settlements of their own, based on such old-country skills as spinning silk and making wine. While not all succeeded, one settlement that did

CRAFTSMAN, ARTIST, PATRIOT

THE BEST-KNOWN HEIR of the Huguenot tradition achieved lasting fame as an American patriot.

Paul Revere was the son of Apollos de Rivoire, a Huguenot refugee and silversmith who Anglicized his name after settling in Boston around 1716. The son continued in the family craft and displayed remarkable talent as an engraver. He also worked as a bellmaker, a dentist, an inventor, and a propagandist. His engraving of the Boston Massacre

publicized British suppression of American liberties and incited strong anti-British sentiments. But Revere made his greatest mark as a volunteer militiaman, when he made the famous midnight ride from Boston to Lexington, Massachusetts, to warn revolutionary leaders that British troops were on the march in April 1775.

TOOLS OF HIS TRADE A silversmith's needle, two engraver's burins, and a hammering pillow are the tools shown in Paul Revere's portrait, painted in the 1760's by John Singleton Copley.

CONVIVIAL EVENING   British officers enjoy brandy and liqueurs after a dinner hosted by Peter Manigault, son of Huguenot merchant and planter Gabriel Manigault of South Carolina, who made his fortune trading colonial deerskins, leather, and foodstuffs for textiles, rum, sugar, and wine. At the time this sketch was made, about 1760, fine houses were not far from the frontier. Three men at this table died later in Indian attacks nearby.

was New Rochelle, outside New York City, founded in 1688 by a group that named the village after their old home of La Rochelle in France. Residents became known for their dyed linen bedspreads and decorative carpets woven out of remnants of old clothes. Their schools also became famous for teaching the French language and social graces to the children of English colonists. A New Rochelle education came to be widely regarded as a mark of rank.

In most cases the Huguenots were rapidly assimilated into predominantly English communities, and they sometimes rose to positions of great prominence. The Bowdoins of Maine, for whom Bowdoin College is named, were descendants of the Huguenot immigrant Pierre Baudoin. Faneuil Hall, the scene of revolutionary meetings that earned it the name of America's "cradle of liberty," was a gift to the city of Boston from the highly successful merchant Peter Faneuil. And one of the most celebrated Bostonians of all, Paul Revere, was the son of a Huguenot silversmith.

Perhaps the place where the Huguenots' identity remained the strongest was South Carolina, whose early proprietors, like those of Pennsylvania, lured settlers by advertising a promise of religious toleration to immigrants of all faiths. The distinctly French flavor in the old houses and gardens of present-day Charleston can be traced to families named Manigault, Gaillard, DeSaussure, Ravenel, Petigru, and others whose early members became prominent businessmen and leaders of society. Henry Laurens, the son of an industrious Charleston saddler, plantation owner, and merchant, served as president of the Continental Congress during the Revolution and was the United States' first unofficial ambassador to England.

In general, however, the Huguenots' most valuable contribution to their communities was simply through the exercise of skills that helped to raise local standards of living and taste.

METROPOLIS ON THE MISSISSIPPI

In the carefully laid-out city of New Orleans, the population was a simmering mix

of frontier ruffians, slaves and free blacks from around the Caribbean, refugees from the slums

of Paris, local Indians, displaced farmers from Nova Scotia, and convent nuns.

FROM THE TIME it was founded, in 1718, the problem for the town with the elegant name of La Nouvelle Orléans was to find settlers who were willing to take up new lives in the Louisiana swamps. Like settlements almost everywhere on the colonial frontier, it was also hampered in its early growth by a shortage of women. Situated on a beautiful stretch of the lower Mississippi, the frontier community had been under way for a few years when its founder, the Sieur de Bienville, Jean Baptiste Le Moyne, wrote to officials in Paris, pleading: "With wives, I will anchor the roving coureurs de bois into sturdy colonists.... Send me wives for my Canadians; they are running in the woods after Indian girls."

Unfortunately for the colonists, the government was slow to respond. By the time Le Moyne's plea was answered, New Orleans was already 10 years old.

Le Moyne had named the settlement in honor of Philippe d'Orléans, who ruled France as Regent to the boy King Louis XIV. The site had been chosen, along with Biloxi Bay and other points along the coast of the Gulf of Mexico, to secure France's hold on the vast territory drained by the Mississippi River, stretching from the Appalachian Mountains to the Rockies, known as Louisiana. The name of Le Moyne himself, a distinguished Canadian-born citizen of New France, also added prestige to the venture. Nevertheless, few people were eager to settle New Orleans. The solution of the French government was to commission a smooth-talking Scottish promoter named John Law. His Company of the West managed to lure a few hundred immigrants from France with grants of land, and a thousand or more sturdy farmers from Germany with additional promises of livestock, seeds, and tools.

Their destination, however, proved to be not the earthly paradise that Law had described, but a humid, low-lying country that swarmed with mosquitoes, where constant rainstorms turned the unpaved roads to mud. In 1719 a flood washed over the town, and three years later a hurricane leveled most of its flimsy, bark-roofed houses, forcing the inhabitants to rebuild.

BEAUTIFUL NEW WORLD
The founding of a New World colony is portrayed as a noble, almost poetic feat in this elaborate broadside(left), published in France to attract people to new sites the government was trying to settle along the Gulf Coast. The landscape confronting those few settlers who were enticed by such propaganda was, in reality, far closer to the scene above.

STOPOVER In 1720, 7,000 settlers passed through this camp at New Biloxi, waiting for small boats that would take them up the Mississippi. Passengers and supplies—salt, flour, candles, wine—were conveyed to shore in flat-bottomed boats from ships anchored in the Gulf. The only permanent structure was the large warehouse, with the hipped roof typical of French colonial construction. Huts for temporary use were made of palmetto.

John Law, meanwhile, having concluded that voluntary methods were too slow, got official permission to comb the alleys and prisons of Paris for undesirables who could be deported to the new colony by force. Shiploads of vagrants, thieves, prostitutes, and military deserters began to arrive at the New Orleans docks, virtually guaranteeing a raucous atmosphere in the young city. A few coureurs de bois floated down the Mississippi on flatboats, looking for fresh opportunities to trade, and hundreds of black slaves were brought from Africa and the West Indies.

As if to compensate for the unruly background of its citizens, New Orleans had an underlying physical order. It grew slowly at first, but steadily, on a grid carefully laid out by French engineers. The plan centered on the spacious Place d'Armes (later renamed Place Royale and, still later, Jackson Square), guarded by a fort at each corner, overlooking the Mississippi River with a vast cypress swamp as its backdrop. The site of the original settlement is famed today as the city's French Quarter, also known as the Vieux Carré, or Old Square. Here, government headquarters and a church, later replaced by a cathedral, were built in due course, along with the Ursuline Convent, which served as a school, an orphanage, and a home to the nuns. Because the first exposed-timber frame constructions

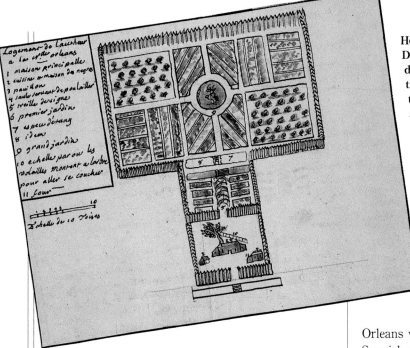

HOME TO ROOST A farmer and merchant, Dumont de Montigny, penned this detailed drawing of his New Orleans home, fenced in the French style, around 1735. An arched trellis covers the path between the house and the main gardens. A ladder placed near the house allows the family's chickens to roost at night in a tree.

the ladies usually had "every other part of their bodies exposed, if not to sight, at least to touch.")

CREOLES AND CAJUNS

By the late 1700's the Place d'Armes had become not only the city's focus, but a veritable crossroads of American colonial life. The leading citizens of New Orleans were the Creoles, a term adapted from the Spanish *criollo*, or native, and applied to persons of French or Spanish extraction, especially those who aspired to the upper class. The Acadians were a group of later French arrivals, mostly peasant farmers and fishermen who had originally settled in Acadia, a region of what is now Nova Scotia. The entire colony had been expelled by the British in 1755, during the French and Indian War. By the 1760's thousands of these outcasts had found their way to Louisiana, where their name was soon corrupted to Cajuns. Arriving with almost nothing, they started life anew in the watery bayou country upriver from New Orleans, raising cattle, rice, cotton, indigo for blue dyes, and sugar cane. Other Cajuns moved westward, crossing the Mississippi to settle in areas of the Atchafalaya swamp and the prairies of southwestern Louisiana.

In the Louisiana back-country, the Cajuns preserved many of their old customs and patterns of speech. Racing ponies was a favorite form of entertainment,

did not last more than a few years in the humid climate, none of the earliest buildings survived.

In 1728 the French government finally addressed the problem of the colony's shortage of women. That year a ship reached New Orleans with the first of several passenger loads of proper young women, called *filles à la cassette* ("casket girls"), because the government had supplied each with a chest of clothes and linens with which to begin their new lives. The girls were lodged together under the watchful eyes of Ursuline nuns and allowed to see suitors only by day, in the presence of armed chaperones. Almost as soon as they arrived, all were whisked off into matrimony.

In 1743 New Orleans got another social lift with the arrival of a new governor, the party-loving Marquis de Vaudreuil, who introduced promenades, banquets, and fancy balls. During his rule four-horse carriages were used in the city for the first time, and the galas he promoted during the pre-Lenten carnival season were the beginnings of the city's famed Mardi Gras. In those years dancing became the passion of the poor as well as the rich. One traveler marveled at the residents: "In the winter they dance to keep warm, and in the summer they dance to keep cool." Others declared that New Orleanians would dance all day and all night if they possibly could. Masked balls were the most popular kind of celebration; a reveler could be bolder when disguised. (One critic noted that covering the face often encouraged uncovering elsewhere, and that

---

BEYOND ENFORCEMENT

In 1723 the citizens of New Orleans showed such a zest for gambling that the town's governing body, the Superior Council, tried to curb it. The council passed a decree forbidding "lasquenet, hoca, biribi, faro, bassett, and all other games of chance or with stakes," even in the home. But the law proved unenforceable.

THE SHOP OF THE FREEDMAN CABINETMAKER

IN EARLY NEW ORLEANS, free people of color were a small but distinctive group, with status lower than that of white citizens but higher than slaves'. Many worked as black- smiths, masons, carpenters, and cabinetmakers. In Louisiana the most striking item of furniture cabinetmakers produced was the French-style armoire, or clothes cupboard, made in fine-grained local woods, like walnut or cherry. The 18th-century armoire depicted here is typical in its elegant simplicity and generous size—about 80 inches high.

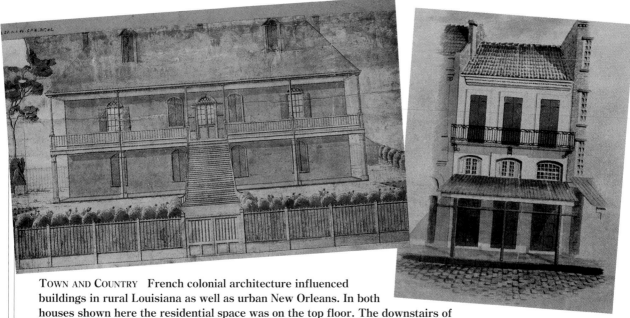

TOWN AND COUNTRY   French colonial architecture influenced buildings in rural Louisiana as well as urban New Orleans. In both houses shown here the residential space was on the top floor. The downstairs of the plantation home at left housed wine cellars and a dining room, and the upstairs was accessible only from an outside staircase. At right, the ground floor served as the commercial quarters, and the third floor was residential. The low-ceilinged middle floor, or *entresol,* was the shopkeeper's residence, or a storage area.

and many communities had a rustic building called the *fais-dodo,* where everyone gathered to dance to fiddle music on Saturday evenings. A Cajun wedding usually meant a huge neighborhood feast, for which the women baked days in advance and the men butchered and barbecued the meats.

In the social ferment of so many influences, New Orleans and its environs developed a unique cuisine from an imaginative blend of French, Spanish, Indian, and African recipes and abundant local produce. Jambalayas were a group of traditional Cajun dishes, involving rice as the basic ingredient combined with meat, fish, or shellfish. Dishes popular among the New Orleans Creoles included fricasees, in which meats were

lightly browned and then made into a stew, and soupy gumbos, named after a West African word for okra, their main ingredient. Many variations on all these have been built around combinations of catfish, crayfish, shrimp, chicken, peppers, red beans, pork, and rice.

THE BLACK CODE

A major factor in shaping the distinctive character of New Orleans and the region was the Code Noir (Black Code), instituted by the government in 1724. A set of laws designed to regulate the conduct of both blacks and whites and to prevent cruelty, the code required masters to feed and clothe their workers properly, to instruct them in the Christian faith, and to care for

A STRANGER'S VIEW OF OKRA

66The table was covered with different dishes and a variety of vegetables, among which the most conspicuous was a large dish of gumbo, served by the hostess at the head, which seemed to be a standing dish and much in repute. It is made

by boiling okra until it is tender and seasoning it with a little bit of fat bacon. It then becomes so ropy and slimy as to make it difficult with either knife, spoon, or fork to carry it to the mouth, without the plate being connected by a long string, so

that it is a most awkward dish to a stranger, who besides, seldom relishes it, but it is a standing dish among the French Creoles.99

A traveler boarding at the Lafayette Hotel of Mme. Legendre, in Baton Rouge.

them in old age. It also imposed severe punishments on any slave who attempted to steal, rebel, or otherwise step out of line.

One widely ignored provision of the code was the ban against the mixing of whites and blacks. Many such unions took place, and the offspring, called mulattos, were often set free by their white fathers. Later generations were known as quadroons or octoroons, according to the proportions of black and white blood in their ancestry. Men in this group often rose to become skilled artisans or other independent professionals; the women became known for their exotic looks—set off at times by a distinctive way of wearing *tignons*, or bandannas, in their hair—and often became the mistresses of leading men of the city. The writer Lafcadio Hearn later observed:

POOR SUITOR

A Cajun boy showed his interest in a girl by visiting her house on Sunday afternoons. The couple was allowed to be alone in the kitchen, with the family just beyond the open door. If the girl wished to show her lack of interest in the boy, she sewed him a very small coat, which she sent to him in an envelope.

"Uncommonly tall were these famous beauties—citrine-hued, elegant of stature as palmettos, lithe as serpents; never again will such types appear on American soil....What figures for designs in bronze!"

Today New Orleans's unique racial heritage is

LE PARC AUX PETITS A Cajun dance at the local *fais-dodo* lasted from evening well into the next day. Off the hall was a room called the "children's park," where children slept, allowing young mothers an evening out. Women kept one fancy dress for these events and saved their dancing shoes from the mud by arriving barefoot. Candles lit the room, hung on chairbacks. By day the "hogscraper" candlesticks were handy for cleaning hides.

reflected in the knowing but casual way its people describe themselves. Whites there use the term Creole to mean white people descended from French or Spanish residents of the colonial period, while blacks use it to mean people of the same period of both black and white or mixed ancestry, and nobody seems bothered by the discrepancy.

A thriving city toward the end of the 18th century, New Orleans had the spirit and tolerance that stood it in good stead through a time of peculiar political events. In 1762 Louis XV, maneuvering to hold Louisiana against the English, ceded the territory to his Bourbon cousin and ally, Charles III of Spain, though the news of the arrangement did not reach the colony until two years later. Though the polyglot town was willing enough to accept a new infusion of Spanish culture, the people of New Orleans deeply resented the imposition of a Spanish governor, who did not actually arrive until 1768. When he did, he was expelled during a brief rebellion and Spain had to send in an army to restore order. Following disastrous fires in 1788 and 1794, the town

MOONLIGHT SERENADE
After a wedding, Cajun revelers would gather under the window of the newlywed couple for a *charivari*—a celebratory mock serenade. Friends and neighbors would shake rattles and beat tin tubs until the bride and groom invited them inside, where the party would continue.

was rebuilt, showing a stronger blend of Spanish and French architectural traditions in the combination of iron filigree, shaded balconies, and courtyards that are the trademarks of New Orleans today.

By that time, however, events to the north, as well as in Europe, had weakened the appeal of the region as a colonial outpost for either Spain or France. On November 30, 1803, the citizens of New Orleans watched as the flag of Spain was lowered in the Place d'Armes and replaced by the new tricolor of Republican France. But President Thomas Jefferson had already arranged for the Louisiana Purchase, and 20 days later, the tricolor yielded to the Stars and Stripes of the United States.

FRENCH SETTLEMENTS
The French lost their major land claims in Canada and the Northeast to the British after the French and Indian War ended in 1763. But French immigrants continued coming to the New World, swelling the ranks of unofficial French communities in Charleston, New York, Boston, and New Orleans.

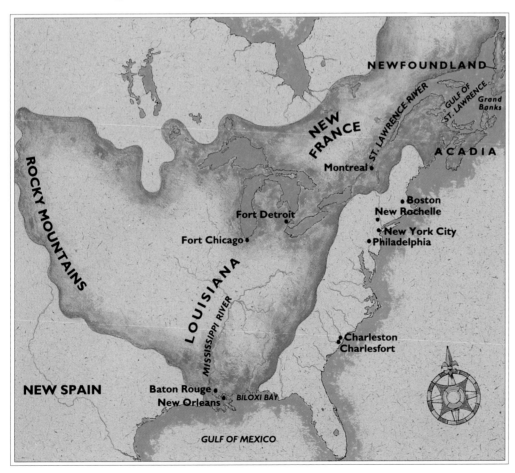

THE PATTERN GROWS RICHER

BIRTH CERTIFICATE IN GERMAN *FRAKTUR* LETTERING, BERKS COUNTY, PENNSYLVANIA

Reports from the colonies of the New World spread across Europe

in the 17th century, attracting different groups for different reasons. The Dutch settled

New Netherland for the rich farmlands along the Hudson River.

The Swedes wanted to develop trade, and Protestants from Germany sought

the freedom to worship in peace. All brought legacies of the Old World that

defined the character of the new societies they created.

A NEW NETHERLAND

During the 17th century, life was so good for most people in Holland that few saw reason

to leave. To strengthen their hold on the great harbor at New Amsterdam and

the Hudson Valley to the north, the Dutch often had to recruit settlers from elsewhere.

DUTCH MERCHANTS began the search for settlers willing to found a colony in the New World in 1609, the year Henry Hudson sailed up the great river that was to bear his name. The English sea captain, on a voyage sponsored by the Dutch, found a region of navigable rivers bounded by fertile lands, and explorers and traders who followed him claimed it as New Netherland. In 1624 three colonies were set up, at Fort Orange (later Albany) and sites on the Connecticut and Delaware Rivers.

In 1626 the island at the mouth of the Hudson was bought for 60 Dutch guilders' worth of trade goods, and New Amsterdam was founded at the southern tip. A tribe of Manhattan Indians, who were farmers and hunters, shared the island with the colonists, about half of whom were Dutch; the rest were Protestant Walloons (from what is now Belgium), Spaniards, Danes, Italians, and Huguenots from France. Elsewhere along the Atlantic coast, a traveler in the mid-17th century was likely to hear only English spoken, except for an occasional word of Algonquian adopted from the Indians or an African dialect spoken among slaves. But on the streets of New Amsterdam in 1643, a French priest counted 18 languages spoken in a population of a few hundred people.

Modeled after its bustling European namesake, New Amsterdam had two broad curved streets, one of which lay alongside a canal; at high water, market goods were poled on barges into town. In winter children skated on the frozen canal, as they did in the old country. Blocks were divided into four-house lots, each of which had a garden plot, a farming strip, and a bit of marsh to provide the salt hay that helped the Hollander cattle to thrive. In the town and beyond were farms for crops as well as *bouweries,* where livestock were raised. Here and there above the horizon, the huge paddles of a windmill turned to grind grain.

Houses were built in the steep Dutch style, of particolored brick and stone, topped with step gables at the end. Roofs were both tiled and thatched. Wooden shutters swung out from the windows, and "Dutch" doors were divided at the top and bottom to let in light and air while keeping animals out. In the main room, the Dutch hearth was not recessed but extended into the room under an overhanging hood. Around the hood rim a cloth ruffle added decoration while helping to guide smoke up the chimney. Blue-and-white delftware pottery, made in Holland, might hang on the walls like pictures, and beds were built into the corners of the room, enclosed in curtained alcoves. The

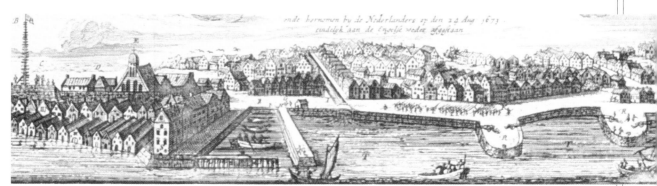

URBAN CENTER   New Amsterdam in 1673, after the Dutch recaptured New Netherland from the English. In this map inset, the battery emplacements are overly large, but the style of the buildings and the layout of lower Manhattan streets are accurate. A treaty signed New Netherland over to the English again within a few months.

MARKET DAY   In 1656 the council of the director general established Saturday as the official Market Day in New Amsterdam. Farmers from up the Hudson River, the bouweries of Brooklyn, and elsewhere nearby set up stalls to sell their garden-fresh produce and dairy goods at the corner of Pearl and Whitehall Streets, south of the fort near the docks. Foreign sailors shopped alongside wharf traders, longshoremen and housewives as everyone sought the services of tailors, barbers, bakers, and wheelwrights like the one repairing a wagon wheel at right.

JUST LIKE HOME Holland was a nation built on sea trade, and its people were accustomed to enjoying imports. Dutch colonial hearths were rimmed with chimney cloths from the home country and tin-glazed tiles from the city of Delft. This room reconstruction at the Brooklyn Museum shows a 1730's Dutch Long Island farmhouse.

most prominent piece of furniture in the home of a wealthy family was often a great carved cupboard called a *kas*, which would hold family clothing and linens and dominate the room. In every Dutch home, whether humble or grand, plank floors were scoured clean and smooth with sand.

New Amsterdam was a company town. The Dutch West India Company, formed in 1621, brought in most settlers and owned the town outright. Acting as the patroon, or feudal-like proprietor, the company oversaw laws passed and enforced by New Amsterdam's local council under the governor, or director general, sent to the colony. The governor's rule extended over all of New Netherland, from Albany southward to the Delaware River, also explored by Hudson in 1609.

In 1625, needing both settlers and laborers, the West India Company began to import African slaves for those citizens who could afford to buy them. A few years later the company offered huge parcels of land to individuals rich enough to act as patroons by financing the immigration of up to 50 tenants. In 1639 a lenient tenant offer, similar to the British system of indenture, was introduced to entice landless farmers: in addition to free passage to the colony, a patroon would supply a working farm stocked with four horses, four cows, sheep, swine,

and tools. In return the tenant would owe an annual rent equivalent to about 80 pounds of butter for six years; at the end of this time the increase in livestock would belong to the tenant, and if he had been thrifty his savings might allow him to buy his own farm. With this inducement the number of bouweries in Manhattan quadrupled in a year, and more settlers came to Staten Island and other nearby areas.

TROUBLED RELATIONS

By the 1640's the Manhattans, Raritans, and other tribes of the Algonquian nation were cornered on small pockets of land that had once all been theirs, with the cows of the newcomers invading their corn fields. The tribes were further angered when the Dutch, who refused to let them have weapons, sold guns to the Iroquois, their historic enemy and tribute-demanding overlords. Then, in 1641, the governor blamed the Raritans for the theft of some pigs from a Dutch farm on Staten Island, and it was enough to set off a war in the region. The population of New Amsterdam swelled as settlers arrived from isolated farms, seeking safety in numbers.

At the same time, the West India Company was encouraging new settlers to establish self-governing towns, and middle-class Dutch farmers and craftsmen, as well as farmers from England and the English colonies, responded. Brooklyn became the first of these autonomous towns, established on Long Island. But in 1647 New Amsterdam was still under strict company control, thanks to Peter Stuyvesant, its governor.

"I shall govern you as a father his children," Stuyvesant wrote that year, "for the advantage of the char-

LINEN PRESS The simple purpose of this elaborately carved oak piece, 76 inches in height, was to press the wrinkles out of clothing and linens.

EXCELLENT SPIRITS Prized Holland gin reached New Netherland in bottles like this one. Beer was the brew usually downed with meals.

tered West India Company, and these burghers, and this land." He showed little appreciation of the variety of citizens under his charge, describing New Amsterdam as "peopled by the scrapings of nationalities." Nevertheless, the diversity of the city's population increased during his leadership, with the arrival of French Waldensian Protestants, Moravians, Scots, English Independents, and Swiss Anabaptists. In 1654 the first Jews arrived, fleeing the risk of another Inquisition after the Portuguese overpowered a colony the Dutch had established in Brazil.

In this thoroughly mixed population, the culture of New Netherland nevertheless remained Dutch. In general, the society was more permissive than the English colonies toward its children, and more egalitarian in its attitude toward women. Boys and girls played together, were taught to read in school, and learned the Calvinist catechisms of the Dutch Reformed Church. In winter children sledded and ice-skated, and in summer they played marbles or rolled hoops in the streets. If they made noise in church, their caps might be confiscated by the warden, a mild punishment requiring that they explain their part in the disturbance to their parents. Preparing for marriage, Dutch girls sewed clothes and linens and stored them as part of their dowry. In contrast to the English, Dutch women could own and inherit property, which enhanced their value in marriage.

DUTCH LIFE IN THE COUNTRY

Upriver on the Hudson, Fort Orange thrived at the hub of the Iroquois fur trade in the midst of a vast patroonship known as Rensselaerswyck. In 1631, Kiliaen van Rensselaer established a claim along eight miles of the river,

extending back from both banks as far as the patroon believed his tenants could manage.

Tenant farmers immigrating into the region were warned to arrive in the spring so that they would have time to build their houses and plant their first crop of grain before the onset of winter. The following spring they built fences, hayricks, and barns, often working side by side with slaves. Farmers threshed wheat and rye, produced cheese and milk, and planted apple and pear trees for future harvests. By 1680 barges loaded with cash crops of meat, bacon, butter, cheese, and vegetables were making their way downriver every Saturday to the New Amsterdam market. The Dutch barns, which supported the many enterprises of farm families, were enormous. In 1697 a traveler, bedded down in a Dutch barn, described a sleepless night marked by the grunting of hogs, squealing of pigs,

BAKED GOODS OF THE HOLIDAYS

THE DUTCH relished their baked goods, in every flavor and shape, stuffed with fruits and nuts, dusted with sugar, braided, twisted into pretzels, made into fruit- or meat-filled pockets called pasteys, or served plain. Religious holidays inspired a spectacular array of cookies, cakes, and loaves. There was some kind of baked good unique to every occasion. With the approach of Saint Nicholas' Day, bake-shop windows displayed *speculaas*, or molded spice cookies. On the eve of the holiday, children left shoes on the hearth to be filled with presents if they had been good, or switches if they had been bad. Good or bad, everyone enjoyed eating a portion of the evening's *duivekater*, a handsome diamond-shaped loaf flavored with currants or raisins that

was served throughout the winter holiday season. Marzipan, raisin rolls, wafers, a long honey-flavored loaf called a *deventer koek*, and candied spices or seeds called comfits were also part of the St. Nicholas celebrations.

At New Year's, people ate tasty *oliekoecken*, the forerunner of the modern doughnut. On Twelfth Night, everyone sang carols and ate waffles. The highlight of this holiday was the crown-shaped loaf called Three Kings Bread, baked with a bean inside. When the loaf was cut the person who received the slice with the bean was crowned king for the night.

Deventer Koek

Duivekater

59

VERSATILE AND WELL MADE: THE DUTCH WAGON

❝You have often admired our two-horse wagons. They are extremely well-contrived and executed with a great deal of skill; and they answer with ease and dispatch all the purposes of a farm. A well-built wagon, when loaded, will turn in a very few feet more than its length.... On a Sunday it becomes the family coach.

We then take off the common, plain sides and fix on it others which are handsomely painted.... Thus equipped, the master of the family can carry six persons either to church or to meetings.... In order to prevent too great shakings, our seats are suspended on wooden springs,— a simple but very useful mechanism.

These inventions and (this) neatness we owe to the original Dutch settlers.... The Dutch build them with timber which has been previously three years under water and then gradually seasoned.❞

A farmer in Orange County, New York, writing in the 1780's.

BUSY HOMESTEAD This wagon, house and hayrick—all characteristically Dutch—were painted in the mid-1700's on the overmantel above the fireplace of the Catskills farmhouse that appears in the scene.

bleating and coughing of sheep, barking of dogs, crowing of cocks, and cackling of hens.

Childhood on the farm could be fun and rollicking, but it was usually short. The children of highborn patroons played with the humbler children of tenants and independent farmers. In less prosperous families, a child might be sent off to another family as an indentured apprentice at about age eight. In the apprenticeship household a girl might spend her time spinning, embroidering, or knitting, while a boy was put to work farming or learning a craft. A boy in his late teens might acquire a load of trade goods to take into the woods to barter with Indians for furs. The money from the fur sale might be used to marry, which Dutch boys often did around the age of 20. Dutch brides wore white, and along with their dowries of linen they might bring a bed to the marriage. If the family of the girl was well-to-do, she might also bring a slave. The wedding was celebrated with wine and a spread of Dutch foods likely to include pear tarts, spiced breads,

and pancakes, and the festivities might last all night.

For a funeral, comforting Dutch traditions often alleviated the sadness of the occasion. A messenger arriving with news of the death of a neighbor would bring such gifts as a white linen scarf, a pair of black silk funeral gloves, a bottle of Madeira, or cakes, and then invite the head of the household to attend the funeral service.

In 1664, there were 10,000 settlers in New Netherland, and 1,600 in New Amsterdam when four English warships arrived in the port. King Charles II wanted to end Dutch power in the region between the English colonies in New England and Virginia, and although war had not been declared, Stuyvesant surrendered the city rather than allow it to be looted. In 1673 the countries were at war when the Dutch retook New Netherland, but a few months later they signed a treaty relinquishing their claim. Still, the region's predominant culture remained Dutch; until 1776, Dutch was the language taught in New York schools.

THE SWEDES AND FINNS

From their forested homelands Swedes and Finns brought skills that left their imprint

on the new land. Wielding axes to build the first log cabins on the continent, or carving out

tableware, stools, and beds, they were masters of the woodworking arts.

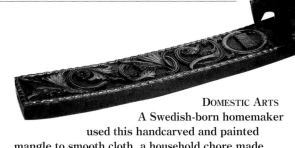

REPORTING ON his 1609 voyage, Henry Hudson declared that the furs of the Delaware Bay were not as good as those available along the Hudson, and that Delaware tobacco was not as fine as that which came from Maryland and Virginia. Nevertheless, Swedish traders wanted ways to recoup their losses in European wars and believed that there were markets for these products. In 1638 they established New Sweden, on what Hudson had called the "River of the South."

A religious edge was added to the colony's goals when Sweden's Royal Council urged Johan Printz, the newly appointed governor, to convert the local Indians to Sweden's version of Protestantism, derived from Martin Luther rather than John Calvin. "Adorn your little church and priest after the Swedish fashion," wrote the president of the council, "with the usual habiliments of the altar, in distinction from the Hollanders and English, shunning all leaven of Calvinism."

Arriving in Delaware Bay in 1643, the almost 400-pound Printz, dubbed "Big Guts" by the Delaware Indians, called in at New Sweden's Fort Christina, on the site of present-day Wilmington. For his own home he chose to live farther north, on an island in the Delaware River, where he built a fort and an earthwork redoubt, flanked by two tobacco plantations on either side of the river. Printz wrote in his report back to Europe:

DOMESTIC ARTS
A Swedish-born homemaker used this handcarved and painted mangle to smooth cloth, a household chore made more pleasant by the lighthearted design.

"Divine service is performed here in the good old Swedish tongue, our priest clothed in the vestments of the Mass on high festivals, solemn prayer-days, Sundays, and Apostles' days precisely as in old Sweden, and differing in every respect from that of the sects around us... All this has long been witnessed by the savages, some of whom we have had several days with us, attempting to convert them; but they have watched their chance, and invariably run off to rejoin their pagan brethren."

A FRUSTRATED GOVERNOR

In the long decade of his governorship, the hearty Printz begged regularly for more colonists, and never got enough. Artisans, soldiers, servants—and especially the unmarried women desired by the unmarried men—were all needed to make the colony a going concern. But Swedes were happy at home, and no more than 200 chose to make the journey. For the first cargo of goods bound for Sweden, Printz managed to collect only 300 beaver pelts locally, and purchased the rest of his total of 2,142 skins from colonies to the north. Much of the 20,467 pounds of tobacco he shipped was bought from his English neighbors to the south.

In 1650 Printz wrote, "Most of the people are alive and well. They are generally supplied with oxen and cattle, and cultivate the land with assiduity, sowing rye and barley, and planting orchards of delicious fruit, and would do better if all had wives and ser-

FLOWERS AND IRON
A loving attention to surface detail is evident in this painted chest, only 24 inches wide. It was brought to New Sweden in 1638.

Houses Hewn from the Forest

THE FOREST-DWELLING ancestry of Swedes and Finns made them highly skilled with the ax. A Swede could "fell 12 of the biggest oaks in a day," claimed one 17th-century colonial observer, and hew the logs into planks with nothing but his ax and a wooden wedge.

The houses these settlers built out of unfinished round logs were ideally suited for the colonial frontier. All that was needed to build one was a pile of logs, notched at the ends, and a little help from the neighbors in stacking the logs into walls. Where the fit between logs

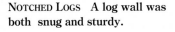

NOTCHED LOGS A log wall was both snug and sturdy.

was not tight the space could be filled with clay or moss; construction also required few nails, which were in short supply in the wilderness.

In the Swedish log house, the chimney was constructed across an end corner, taking advantage of the adjoining walls to minimize construction. In substantial houses built in 17th-century Sweden the corner fireplace was usually square, with the hearth about 12 inches off the floor, and extended into the room under a hood. In New Sweden, fireplaces were usually built straight across the corner and faced into the room on the diagonal.

EVOLVING TOOL The handle of this 17th-century ax lacks the curve that adds accuracy and heft to axes made today.

SWEDISH CHIMNEY The colonial corner version was rustic.

The founder of Pennsylvania, William Penn, was so impressed by the efficiency of the Swedish log houses that he encouraged German settlers to follow the model. It was the Scotch-Irish who spread the use of the log house in the 18th century, into Maine and New Hampshire, then down through the Alleghenies. By 1770 the log house was known in Virginia as the "log cabin," and was on its way to becoming the most lasting symbol of the American frontier.

vants. Last year the crops were particularly excellent, our freemen having a hundred tons of grain to sell."

But Printz's efforts and optimistic wishes weren't enough to make it prosper. He became discouraged, and he missed his native country. In 1653, he asked to be recalled to Sweden, where he returned with his wife and five children.

While the Swedes were mostly content with their society, sharing their Lutheran traditions without dissent, their community did have a struggling minority. Their underclass was the Finns, whose country had been absorbed by the Swedes during the Middle Ages. Unemployed and homeless Finns roamed Sweden's iron-mining areas looking for work, and sometimes incurred Swedish wrath by burning off valuable timber while clearing land for cultivation. When Sweden needed New World settlers, vagrant Finns and forest-burners were forced to emigrate and tilled the land around Delaware Bay for a few years until they could regain the status of free men. Both Swedes and Finns were skilled in lumbering and built their houses out of

logs. Because walls could only be as long as the available logs, their way of increasing the size of living space was to build a second room, or house, connected to the first by a breezeway.

In their native woods, the Swedes had also developed woodworking to a fine art. The colonists brought with them clothing and table linens packed in wooden chests and fashioned tableware, drinking cups, cradles, and stools out of wood. For their new homes they built wooden beds, trestle tables, and chairs. They built log fences three rails high around their crops.

In 1654 Swedes captured the Dutch settlement at Fort Casimir. The following year Peter Stuyvesant retaliated by invading New Sweden, with seven ships and 350 soldiers, and Fort Christina fell after a short siege. The Dutch declared sovereignty over all of New Sweden, but the Swedish colonists were allowed to stay. Three decades later, well after the Dutch had lost their New World dominion to the British, land was still owned by Swedish farmers, including the first acreage bought by William Penn.

THE PENNSYLVANIA GERMANS

Groups of Germans, led by a visionary Englishman named William Penn, left behind

wartorn lands to pursue their spiritual dreams in the New World and

bring their exceptional skill and energy to farming, business, and a myriad of crafts.

IT WAS THE VISION OF the young English Quaker William Penn that first drew Germans to the Delaware region to settle in large numbers. In his twenties Penn traveled in Germany as a missionary with the Quaker founder, George Fox, and preached about a city of brotherly love. In 1681, when Penn was 37, he was made proprietor of an enormous tract of land along the west bank of the Delaware River, to cancel a debt owed by England's King Charles II to Penn's father. Shortly afterward, Penn began to sell off plots of the unsurveyed land, fulfill-

ing a dream of founding a colony based on Quaker ideals, which included religious freedom, prompt justice through open courts and jury trials, pacifism, individual equality, and separation of church and state. Irish and Welsh Quakers joined the English in buying land sections, as well as Anglicans and Presbyterians; Baptists and Anabaptists were attracted to the venture from all over northern Europe, as well as Mennonites from the region of the Rhine, and other Protestant German sects, making Pennsylvania's population the most diverse of all the American colonies.

UNITED WE STAND A 1757 engraving shows a group wedding of Moravian couples before their departure for America. Letters distinguish couples from unwed members of the pacifist Protestant sect, standing at the rear. Music was part of their daily religious observance; this pipe organ was installed at Bethlehem in 1776.

The German newcomers—mostly shopkeepers, farmers, and craftsmen who followed the traditions of skills dating back to the medieval era—kept their old language and culture and resisted adapting to English colonial ways. In areas of German settlement, street signs were painted in both German and English, or simply in German. In an uncharacteristic show of bias, Benjamin Franklin once wrote: "Why should the Palatine Boors [Germans from the Baden-Palatinate on the Rhine] be suffered to swarm into our Settlements, and by herding together establish their Language and Manners to the exclusion of ours?... Why should Pennsylvania, founded by the English, become a

SECRETS OF SUCCESS

A German farmer who bought a new pig would back the animal into its pen to guarantee it a life of good health. If a Swedish farmer sold a healthy cow he would keep a hank of its hair so that the animal's good luck would not depart with it.

Colony of Aliens, who will shortly be so numerous as to Germanize us instead of our Anglifying them?" It would probably be no surprise to him that in the 1990 census, more Americans proved to have German ancestry than any other.

EPHRATA: SOCIETY OF THE SOLITARY

THE SOCIETY OF THE SOLITARY was typical of a number of small religious sects drawn to Pennsylvania by the colony's religious tolerance. In the shelter of their communities, members devoted themselves to ardent religious practice and labored hard to make their communities self-sufficient.

Ephrata Cloister was the offshoot of a larger Protestant German sect, the Dunkards, founded in Westphalia in 1708, whose religious practices included baptism by total immersion. In 1732, a group left Germany under the leadership of Conrad Beissel to found the community of Ephrata, named after the word meaning "plentiful" in Hebrew.

Beissel's followers were divided into two celibate groups—a sisterhood and a brotherhood—and a third group of married "householders." All lived in barn-like buildings similar to medieval-style houses they had left behind in Germany, and followed regimens of prolonged spiritual meditation. The dormitory buildings housed a kitchen and a common room on each floor, and rows of small rooms where members slept on narrow benches.

Working 12 hours a day, the members produced their own food, made their own clothes and furnishings, and ran various milling operations as well as a printing press. Members of the sisterhood practiced highly skilled calligraphy, and the Ephrata choir sang hymn composed by Beissel as expressions of piety.

In 1750 the society's membership reached 300, but it dwindled rapidly after Beissel's death in 1768. The surviving membership was eventually incorporated into the German Baptist Church. Today much of the Ephrata Cloister has been restored to its 18th-century appearance.

EPHRATA KITCHEN The rough brick floors, plain walls, and spare communal benches and table all offer testimony to the simple lifestyle led by the Society of the Solitary.

GREAT BARN The vast size of an 18th-century Pennsylvania German stone barn is not lost against the backdrop of hills in this contemporary watercolor. The farmer entered on the high side, where the grain was stored. Animals' stalls opened on the downhill side.

The French-born traveler and diarist Hector St. John de Crèvecouer saw the Germans differently: "The honest Germans ... they hire themselves to some of their wealthy landsmen, and in that apprenticeship learn everything that is necessary.... They launch forth, and by dint of sobriety, rigid parsimony, and the most persevering industry, they commonly succeed."

Penn began the sale of his land before he had even left England. His intention was to put his first town upriver from Wilmington, at what is now Chester, Pennsylvania. Many Swedes already held title there, however, and according to the rules of the land grant, if property within it was surveyed and registered, the proprietor was obligated to buy up that portion to claim ownership. In 1682, after he arrived in the colony, Penn chose a new town site farther to the west, past where the Schuylkill River entered the Delaware. It was an area inhabited by 4,000 Algonquians of the Delaware tribe, to whom Penn offered payment. For the respect shown them by the proprietor, these non-aggressive Indians rewarded the settlers in the region with a long-standing peace.

The land for sale was divided into sections comprising 15,000 acres for farming, a house plot in the town that was still to be built, and a dividend of 80 acres in the "liberty lands" north and south of the town. Before the new-comers could construct homes, some lived in caves along the

DIPPING CANDLES
The candlemaker (in the dress here of a member of the Society of the Solitary) dipped her wicks many times before the candles were made. If the wax was too cool the candles were lumpy; if too warm, the layers melted off. Wax from berries of the bayberry bush made pleasantly scented green tapers.

65

CHURCH SERVICE   A scene
of vibrant activity underlies this supposedly quiet
moment during a Lutheran sermon in York,
Pennsylvania. Numerous details of architecture and
life preserved beyond the colonial period have
survived through the watercolors of Lewis Miller.

steep banks of the Delaware. Their daylight hours
were spent cutting through a dense forest of walnut,
chestnut, pine, and spruce. The style of their town
was set when they discovered clay appropriate for making bricks. They built kilns and
began turning out the building materials
for their future houses, public buildings,
and streets.

As the town of Philadelphia grew, its craftsmen set up gristmills, paper mills, glassworks,
and metal shops. Although a long way inland,
at the north end of the Delaware Bay, the town
had a deep river basin offering excellent opportunities for development as a port. Merchants

exported flour, meal, and barrel staves,
rapidly making Philadelphia into a real
boomtown. By 1700 it had 400 houses
and 2,200 residents.

CRAFTS PLAIN AND FANCY

From Philadelphia, German and Dutch
settlers of various sects fanned out
into the countryside, over the area that
would become Lancaster County.
Germans built log cabins and white-
washed the mortar between the logs
on the inside, giving the walls a
striped effect. They made walnut
furniture, which appeared to be
inlaid—the "ivory" material actually a clever mix of beeswax and
powdered white lead. Near their
small houses they built magnifi-
cent barns, with ground stories of
stone and upper stories of vertical
boards, decorated with colorful
symbols. On their farms they produced corn, wheat, barley, butter,
cheese, beef, pork, and fresh fruit
for Philadelphia's dock markets.

Experienced at surviving on small bits of
land in Europe, the colonists now labored with the same
intensity over 15,000-acre tracts, building up prosperous farms overlooking huge expanses of rich tilled soil.

Wherever Germans settled, new forms of craftsmanship flourished. In Lancaster County the Elizabeth
Furnace was set up to produce colored glassware as
well as cast-iron plates to be assembled into stoves that
rested on legs and were set against the chimney flue.
The molded iron surfaces were decorated with heraldic
motifs depicting the doings of Protestant saints or
scenes from Eden. Potters in the region
shaped the local red clay into tableware,
thinned the clay to make an outer layer, or
"slip," then scratched designs through the
slip, which might be yellow, red, green, or
blue. They decorated the dishes with tulips,
unicorns symbolizing virginity, paired birds
for love, doves for conjugal bliss, peacocks for

LOCKSMITH'S WORK   A Moravian door
handle made of brass combines amusing
shape with fine workmanship.

resurrection, and pomegranates for fertility and regeneration.

With the exception of the tulip, which had been introduced relatively recently from Turkey, the decorative symbols could all be traced to medieval Europe. The people repeated them in their whimsical paintings called *fraktur*, using the "broken" lettering combined with pictures and designs to render documents such as birth or marriage certificates as keepsakes, or to decorate a favorite piece of religious music. While Philadelphia gradually grew into a sophisticated town, country Germans preserved their traditionalist and homey thoughts and ways through such crafts. On a baptismal certificate might be written "I am baptized! I am in the covenant Through Baptism with my God." On a piece of pottery might be etched "Rather would I single live than my wife the breeches give."

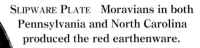

SLIPWARE PLATE Moravians in both Pennsylvania and North Carolina produced the red earthenware.

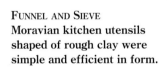

FUNNEL AND SIEVE Moravian kitchen utensils shaped of rough clay were simple and efficient in form.

COMMUNITIES OF THE SPIRIT

Philadelphia and the surrounding counties continued to draw German Protestants. Many settlers came as members of small groups— Amish, Dunkards, Schwenkfelders— bound by their special outlook and convictions. Just outside Philadelphia, a group of Dutch and German Mennonites set up a community at Germantown. To the west, the town of Ephrata was established as a monastic order of German mystics, and Moravians founded Bethlehem, with its particular version of agrarian communism. The Moravian and Ephrata communities were especially musical given to singing in choirs and performing on organs, violins, oboes, clarinets, and flutes.

The mainstream of German immigration brought Lutherans and members of the German Reformed Church. Most came to Pennsylvania, but there were some who went to the colony of Georgia, which James Edward Oglethorpe had established in 1733. Oglethorpe, a member of the British Parliament and a philanthropist, wanted to establish a colony in North America that would offer a second chance

THE FESTIVE DRINK CALLED FLIP

MANY COLONISTS enjoyed mixing their liquors, and drinks were often sweet. One concoction that dated from the 17th century was a heady and pungent brew called flip. Beer was mixed with sugar or some other sweetener (often molasses, since it was cheap), and a stronger spirit such as rum. A red-hot iron was plunged into the mix, making the liquor foam, and tinged its flavor with the bitterness of burnt sugar.

A distinctive wide-mouthed glass became associated with drinking flip. Engraved and enameled versions were imported from Europe, and also produced by the glassworks at Manheim, Pennsylvania, in the 18th century. As the colonial mood turned revolutionary, the poet John Trumbull identified the drink with the rising spirit of patriotism:

GLASSES FOR FLIP Enameled designs set a celebrative mood.

While briskly to each patriotic lip
Walks eager round the inspiring flip
Delicious draught! whose powers inherit
The quintessence of public spirit.

for the disadvantaged, such as convicts, poor people, and debtors. The Georgia colony was also a refuge where all Protestants, no matter what language they spoke or where they came from, could escape religious persecution in Europe.

The Georgia colony was founded on high moral principles that appealed to the Lutherans: the slave trade and the buying and selling of alcohol were both forbidden there. Other rules restricting the ownership and exchange of land were also enforced. But German traditions and cultural influences did not take root and thrive in Georgia as they did in Pennsylvania. Many settlers found the rules too strict and moved to other colonies.

PROGRESS IN PHILADELPHIA

A young Scottish physician named Alexander Hamilton (not the politician) wrote of stopping at Philadelphia during a trip he made from Annapolis to Boston in June 1744: "At my entering the city, I observed the regularity of the streets....The heat in this city is excessive, the sun's rays being reflected with such power from the brick houses and from the street pavement which is brick. The people commonly use awnings of painted cloth or duck over their shop doors and windows and, at sunset, throw buckets full of water upon the pavement which gives a sensible cool."

Philadelphia was enjoying a building boom. The elegant Anglican Christ Church was under construction, and houses were being built on specu-

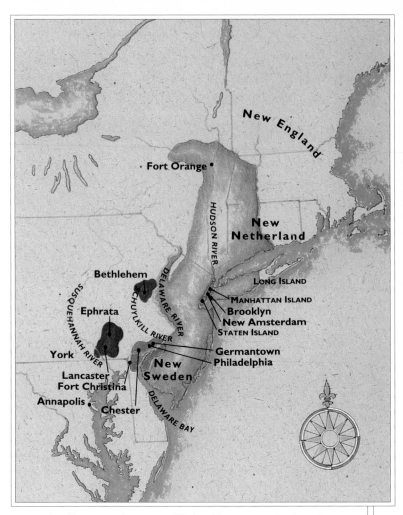

CULTURAL OVERLAP Wedged between colonies of English origin, the Dutch kept their ways of life long after New Netherland became New York. Swedish influence faded after the Dutch took Fort Christina, but was revived in the Great Lakes region in the 19th century. Germans spread from their first settlements (in dark blue) to become the largest immigrant group.

PLAYFUL GIFT The whimsical painting of an 18th-century man on this wooden box matches the style of the uniformed figure in the fraktur on page 55. Such boxes were used as gifts. The one above, 16 inches long, has a tulip motif on the rim.

lation. Hamilton found the people polite but was disappointed in the absence of night life. "I never was in a place so populous where the *gout* for publick gay diversions prevailed so little. There is no such things as assemblys of the gentry among them, either for dancing or musick; these they have had an utter aversion to ever since [the evangelistic Methodist] Whitefield preached among them." Nevertheless the visitor was optimistic about Philadelphia's potential, concluding, "But I believe that in a few years hence it will be a great and a flourishing place and the chief city in North America."

Hamilton's intuition was correct: Philadelphia's population overtook New York's in the 1750's and Boston's in the 1770's.

PLANTERS AND PIONEERS

TIDEWATER VIRGINIA PLANTATION BY AN UNKNOWN FOLK ARTIST

Driven by a hunger for land they never owned in Europe,

settlers eagerly carved farms out of the wilderness, worked backbreaking hours,

raised families, and cultivated the simple pleasures of rural and village life.

In the South, self-made aristocrats presided over great plantations,

while hardy pioneers breached the Appalachian Mountains and arrived in

Kentucky to make new lives on the Western frontier.

LIFE ON THE ROAD

Travelers moved between isolated communities by horse or stagecoach,

stopping at inns and taverns for food, sociability, and a good night's rest. Post riders galloped

from town to town bringing eagerly awaited news and greetings.

THE FIRST SETTLEMENTS in the colonies were so few and far between, and transportation so crude, that it took a very long time just to get from one place to another. Travelers usually journeyed on foot, or in a lumbering ox cart. A fortunate few traveled by horse. As trails widened into rutted wagon tracks, travel slowly improved. By 1732 a wagon carried passengers between Philadelphia and New York; the trip took a week, including ferries at each end. In the 1760's a special coach dubbed "The Flying Machine" cut the time to a breakneck two days. Regardless of speed, riding any such conveyance was a crowded, bumpy, harrowing ordeal.

Long journeys by coach required frequent stops, or "stages," to change teams of horses and to allow tired travelers to get something to eat and a bed for the night. Accommodations between towns at first were limited to a few rural homes licensed as "ordinaries,"

BED & BREAKFAST A coach sets off from the Old Spread Eagle Inn near Lancaster, Pennsylvania. Although the building was rustic, an overnight stay could be a convivial affair, as guests relaxed before dinner with a hot drink in front of an open fire and local citizens gathered to glean the travelers' news of distant places. Tavern signs such as the one from Stranger's Resort in Connecticut (inset) represent American folk art at its best.

Philadelphia STAGE-WAGGON, and New-York STAGE BOAT performs their Stages twice a Week.

JOHN BUTLER, with his wag-
gon, fets out on Mondays from his Houfe, at the Sign
of the Death of the Fox, in Strawberry ally, and drives the
fame day to Trenton Ferry, when Francis Holman meets
him, and proceeds on Tuefday to Brunfwick, and the paffengers and goods being fhifted into the waggon of Ifaac
Fitzrandolph he takes them to the New Blazing Star to
Jacob Fitzrandolph's the fame day, where Rubin Fitzrandolph, with a boat well futed, will receive them, and
take them to New-York that night. John Butler returning to Philadelphia on Tuefday with the paffengers and
goods delivered to him by Francis Holman, will again fet
out for Trenton Ferry on Thurfday, and Francis Holman,
&c. will carry his paffengers and goods, with the fame expedition as above to New-York.   Tcctf.

FERRY SERVICE The tedium of travel from New York to Philadelphia, by wagon and ferry, is suggested in this 18th-century advertisement.

DINNER SET The well-equipped traveler sometimes carried his own set of dinner utensils rather than depend on an inn to provide the tableware.

Observed one surprised traveler: "You meet with neatness, dignity, and decency, the chambers neat, the sheets clean, supper passable, cyder, tea, punch, and all for 14 pence a head."

Many of the stopping places rejoiced in proper English names like The Green Dragon, The Black Horse, The Blue Bell, or The Golden Lion, proclaimed in colorful signs over their doors. With the approach of the Revolution, however, when these same taverns became the scene of protest meetings, British lions and crowns were painted over with eagles or other patriotic motifs. One proprietor even managed to transform the hated King George into a credible likeness of George Washington.

Taverns also served as social centers for local residents, who met regularly to discuss the weather, complain about crops or taxes, and press traveling visitors for news of the outside world.

where one shared whatever the owner happened to have on the table for dinner, and accepted an extra bed in a corner—or the hayloft over the barn.

With the advent of regular stagecoach service, commercial inns and taverns began to appear along major roadways, offering food, drink, and a night's rest.

HOW THE MAIL GOT THROUGH

MUCH VALUED by news-hungry citizens—and idolized by small boys—were the dashing post riders who carried the mail or "post" between colonial towns, stopping at designated taverns to pick up and deliver letters, which were generally thrown on a table until the recipients claimed them.

One of the first regular mail circuits was established in 1673 by riders galloping between New York and Boston, a one-week's journey even for skilled horsemen and double that in winter. (Their route through Connecticut, now U.S. 1, is still known as the Boston Post Road.)

These forerunners of the U.S. Postal Service were not only entrusted with personal and business documents; they were expected to cram bulky packages into their saddle-

MAIL CALL The post rider sounds his horn to announce his arrival in a colonial town.

MILESTONE Post riders charged by the mile; roadside milestones helped them calculate the price of sending a letter or package.

28 Miles
To Bofton.
Right hand
Road to Worcefs
Left hand TO
Graftown

bags, relay spoken messages to friends, and assist travelers in trouble along the road. Their feats live on in the famous postal motto: "Neither snow, nor rain, nor heat, nor gloom of night stays these couriers from the swift completion of their appointed rounds."

VILLAGERS AND FARMERS

Colonial life centered on individual farms, and on small towns where

artisans applied their trades and merchants sold their wares. Farmers had an especially

hard life at first, and many men and women died young as a result.

SMALL SETTLEMENTS that grew up at key points along roads and waterways were the centers of rural life in the colonies. A typical New England village—many are still admired for their architectural beauty and orderly sense of community—took shape around a central common, so called because it was communal land where any resident could graze his cows or sheep. With the constant trampling of hooves, it could be a very muddy place.

When animals grew too numerous, they were relegated to pastures outside town. The common became a parklike greensward where townsfolk and farmers could mingle, and where the volunteer militia could train and parade. This village green would continue to be a much-cherished heart of the community—a tree-shaded locale of band concerts and church fairs, and a place for a fountain, statues, and war memorials celebrating the town's history.

The most important building on a New England green was the meetinghouse, which at first was used for both church services and town meetings. Early meetinghouses were plain structures with low, blocky bell towers; only when congregations built their own separate churches did tall, graceful steeples appear, expressing man's aspiration to heaven.

As the villages prospered and grew into towns, the homes of leading citizens were built along the green. Many boasted fine windows, doorways, and other

MARKET SHED In Germantown, Pennsylvania, the open marketplace was the focal point of village life. At left, the gray building with dormer windows is typical of fieldstone houses built by many settlers in the region.

architectual details. Nearby, on the main street or down side alleys, were the necessities of village life: the shops of artisans and merchants, which often served as their homes as well.

In the smithy, a muscular, sweating blacksmith heated pieces of iron in a charcoal fire—kept going by his apprentice with a huge, puffing bellows—then hammered the red-hot metal into horseshoes, ox shoes, farm tools, andirons, latches, hinges, and nails. In the absence of dentists, he also obliged distressed citizens by pulling aching teeth with his tongs.

In the cobbler's shop, the village shoemaker fashioned shoes and boots to order. A customer placed his foot on a piece of leather, and the cobbler drew the outline, cutting and sewing soles and uppers together and fastening the heels with wooden pegs. The finished product could be worn on either foot.

Down the street might be the shop of a carpenter or "joiner," who made coffins, chests, tables, chairs, and other furniture. As the 18th century progressed, the best carpenters became specialized as cabinetmakers.

Somewhat removed from the village, because of the odors that emanated from the enterprise, was the tannery, where farmers brought their hides to be made into leather. Along a rushing stream inside or outside of town was usually a gristmill, where a waterwheel turned a millstone that ground farmers' wheat, rye, and corn into flour. There might also be a sawmill, with a water-powered saw that transformed logs into boards, and a fulling mill, which finished the woolens that housewives made at home.

Items that villagers were unable to produce for themselves were brought to town by traveling peddlers, whose wagons were crammed with tinware, kettles, pots, clocks, scissors, fancy cloth, combs, pins, needles,

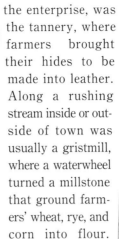

COPPER KETTLE
The coppersmith hammered out goods from sheet metal. This kettle's deep handle allowed it to hang over the hearth on a crane.

VILLAGE SMITHY
Blacksmiths cast and wrought metal, mostly iron, to produce objects like the door hinge (above) and the down-hearth toaster (left), used to place slices of bread close to the flames.

ARTISANS PAYING TAXES IN GERMANTOWN, PENNSYLVANIA, IN 1773	
Fabric crafts	
Stocking weaver	20
Weaver	11
Tailor	12
Hatter	6
Dyer	4
Leather crafts	
Cordwainer	17
Tanner	10
Saddlemaker	8
Skinner	7
Food	
Butcher	10
Miller	6
Baker	4
Metal crafts	
Blacksmith	11
General crafts	
Clockmaster	5
Bookbinder	3
Painter	3
Printer	2
Woodworking and building	
Cooper	26
Mason	10
Carpenter	9
Joiner	8
Transportation	
Coachmaker	8
Carter	8
Wheelwright	6

TAX ROLLS Demand for skilled labor was high in the colonies, and artisans could earn good wages. Artisans in many communities owned enough property to qualify as voters in local elections.

and just about everything else. Itinerant craftsmen—shoemakers, tailors, tinkers, and chandlers—also traveled from village to village.

Like the tavern, the general store became an informal center of village life, a place where folks could buy anything from pitchforks and horsewhips to candy and soap—or just drop in to socialize with the proprietor and the neighbors.

DOWN ON THE FARM

In New England and elsewhere, the men and women who laid the foundations of America were mostly farmers; in 1760, a full 90 percent of all residents in the colonies still relied for their primary living on the soil. For many of them, life was no pastoral idyll; it was a struggle to survive. Not all did. A poignant note is contained in a letter a young wife wrote to her parents in Boston: "It was in the summer of the 2nd yeare that my Johne dyed of the worke."

The "worke" required a strong back and stout heart. Land was relatively easy to come by, but in many areas it was covered with dense forest, which first had to be cleared. It was an arduous task to fell the trees with crude broad axes, then drag them off with the help of an ox or horse, cut them into firewood and building material, and, if possible, pry up the large root systems and stumps. In northern areas, where ancient glaciers had dropped their rocky burdens, it also meant digging countless boulders out of the earth and piling them into stone walls.

QUAKER FARM The prosperous 18th-century farm was a veritable village in itself, as shown in this work by Quaker folk artist Edward Hicks. Note the English-style plow, in contrast to the Dutch plow below.

Only when these labors were done could a farmer begin to plow his fields and plant his crops. Poor soil or bad weather, however, could cut his yields below expectations; disease, insects, or hungry deer could wipe out a crop overnight; back strain or accidental injury could put the farmer himself out of action for weeks. Little wonder that farm families described their lives as "working from can to can't, and still nothing to show for it."

Another old saying got its start in those days: "From early morn to setting sun, woman's work is never done." Much of a farm woman's life focused on keeping her family fed, and when not preparing the day's meals, she had plenty of other tasks. She sheared sheep, cleaned and carded the wool, spun it into yarn, and wove it into warm clothing for her family to wear. She milked the cows, drew water from the well, butchered livestock, smoked meat and fish, and harvested vegetables and stored some of them in her root cellar for winter use. If she had a household servant or slave, there would be plenty to keep them busy, too. In the midst of the chores, she also found time to bear and raise children. And when they or her husband got sick, she acted as the family doctor, relying on traditional housewives' remedies that sometimes worked and often did not.

WHEELED PLOW This Dutch design worked best on flat land.

Once a farm was established and running to its own rhythms, however, the owners usually found time for other pursuits. By its nature, farm work was sporadic. Plowing and planting consumed weeks of hard labor in spring, as did harvesting in summer and fall. During the growing season, however, there was sometimes less to do, leaving days free for fishing, hunting, loafing, or visiting friends. In tobacco-growing country, the down time was usually a few months in the dead of winter.

In colder climates, late summer and fall usually meant splitting logs for the huge woodpile that winter would require. Winter weather often limited outdoor activities—except for constant trips to the woodpile to replenish the fire (one observer estimated that the average farmer spent 40 percent of his working hours from October through March in gathering wood). At almost any time of year, farmers occupied themselves with needed tasks such as repairing barns or fences, making simple furniture, or riding to town to get supplies or to sell surplus cows, hides, or grain.

Since farming could be a precarious living, most farm families tried to supplement their incomes with a sideline or two that would carry them through leaner years. When his regular chores ended, a farmer who was adept at carpentry might hire himself out to build a house addition or a shed. A man who had learned the basics of blacksmithing often shod his neighbors' horses or put new iron rims on their wagon wheels. One with a bent for leatherworking might not only make items for his own family but would also offer fancy belts, gloves, or moccasins for sale.

In the northern colonies, a farm wife could sometimes use her sewing, knitting, or weaving skills to gain extra income by contracting to do "piecework" for a traveling entrepreneur with a little extra money to invest as a trader in handwork she wanted to sell. The woman would fit the work into the hours she was keeping an eye on the

EVERYDAY DRESS
Women usually wore a fitted bodice over a skirt called a petticoat.

pot over the fire or younger children, and when the trader returned on his rounds to pick up her completed work he would bring her a fresh supply of wool, linen, or other raw materials that she would turn into more goods by the next time he came around again. If the woman had an older daughter or two to whom she had passed along her skills, mother and daughters together could turn out a considerable volume of work.

In reverse fashion, village craftsmen often kept a hand in farming to hedge their economic bets. Artisans would own and cultivate fields on the outskirts of town, maintaining livestock to produce salable milk, cheese, eggs, meat, or hides. Millers and tanners, who normally plied their trades at a distance from the town center, might own land around their places of work. Village merchants also found fertile land to be a sound investment. If they did not farm it themselves, they leased it to tenant farmers or held it in reserve against the day when their business ventures might suffer a setback or fail.

FARM TIPS
The many tasks of the country housewife reflected in this frontispiece suggest how welcome such a self-help book would be. This volume was published in London in 1736.

75

BUILDING FAMILIES

Courtships, marriage, and childbearing followed prescribed and predictable patterns.

Romance was secondary to the economics of marriage, and parents exercised considerable authority

over the choice of a partner. The discipline of children lessened as the century proceeded.

I N THE EIGHTEENTH century life tended to be short and uncertain, and young men and women were expected to get on with the business of raising families. Young women usually married in their late teens or early twenties, and the men waited until they reached legal majority at age 21. Because wedlock was regarded as a serious matter, the choice of partners was made with strong parental guidance. For parents with aspirations for their children, wealth and social standing were more important than love.

By custom, and often by law, a suitor first had to get permission to woo his sweetheart from her father, who could say no if he found the youth unsuitable, and could withhold any dowry to make his point.

If the would-be husband passed this first test, he immediately faced a second: Where could he find enough privacy to murmur sweet nothings in her ear? In summer, a lad and lass might slip away after the day's chores to meet beside the bank of a pretty stream. On a cold winter's eve, however, such a setting was far from romantic, and the family fireside, while warm and cozy, generally had too many relatives hovering around.

One solution, popular in New England, was the custom of "bundling." The young man and woman, both fully clothed—and with parental approval—lay down in a bed, that was sometimes divided in the middle by a "bundling board," which, in theory, served to keep them apart. Then they were left there to exchange thoughts and endearments—without

COLONIAL COURTSHIP A young couple finds a rare moment alone on the banks of the Schuylkill River near Philadelphia in this folk painting done around 1750. Dancing was highly popular, and allowed courting in public.

going any further. Bundling was also practiced by families when beds were scarce for overnight guests. By the late 1700's, bundling began to go out of fashion, probably because the participants—including less scrupulous British soldiers stationed in the colonies—were not so careful to abide by the rules. Preachers denounced the practice from their pulpits as a mortal sin, and for better or worse this unique method of courting disappeared.

After a successful courtship, a wedding day was set. If the families of the couple were not prosperous the ceremony would be as simple and practical as the people themselves. The groom and bride simply joined hands before a civil magistrate or clergyman, who read a few lines and pronounced them man and wife. In prosperous homes there might be much celebration, in the form of a lively party with music, dancing, food, and drink.

When a young wife became pregnant, she was dependent on female relatives or neighbors for the wisdom and comfort they could pass on about her

CRADLE TO GRAVE A somber view of women's lot was stitched into *The First, Second, and Last Scenes of Mortality,* by a young woman named Prudence Punderson. Her intuition proved right: she died nine months after her marriage.

condition, and she would probably have to continue a full load of work in her new home right up until it was time to give birth.

When a woman went into labor, she simply delivered in her own bed, again with the help of a female relative or neighbor. If an experienced midwife was nearby, the woman might be called in to help. Though her techniques were not scientific, the midwife who knew her business could be helpful in delivery.

Little was known about the dangers of infection, however, and when a woman died following childbirth it was usually due to "childbed fever," contracted because the hands of the midwife had been unclean. Before the mid-1700's, doctors rarely attended at routine births, and midwives were considered more knowledgeable about the birth process. Doctors gradually gained expertise through experience and the use of instruments such as forceps.

After her first child, a wife could look forward to another, and another, and another. Large families were the rule, partly to offset the high mortality rate from numerous diseases—less than half of all children reached the age of 16—and partly to ensure a supply

HOPE CHEST As soon as a young girl learned to sew she began to make nightgowns, bed linens, and other items to take into marriage as her "bride wealth," or dowry. Pennsylvania Dutch girls filled decorated dowry chests.

of free labor on the family farm. To have 10 or 12 children was not unusual; an early governor of Massachusetts, William Phips, was one of 26. One New England matriarch died in 1742 leaving behind only 5 children, but 61 grandchildren, 182 great-grandchildren, and 12 great-great-grandchildren.

A CHILD'S WORLD

Children in the colonies were raised under very strict discipline, although permissiveness increased during the 18th century. Boys and girls were expected to do their household and farm chores without question, mind their manners, fear God, and address their elders with respect. If they didn't follow these rules, they soon felt the sting of a paddle or switch.

Depending on family circumstances, education consisted of learning simple ABCs and Bible readings at home or in a school for the poor, lessons in the kitchen of a "dame's school" run by a part-time teacher, or long days in a one-room schoolhouse maintained by the community.

In a typical New England schoolroom in winter, children squirmed and shivered on narrow, backless benches, looked longingly at the crackling fireplace behind the teacher, and fervently wished they were somewhere else. Penalties were frequent and severe. Inattentive pupils were made to wear "whispering sticks," wooden gags that resembled a

RULES for BEHAVIOUR, 1787

CHILDREN'S BEHAVIOUR at the TABLE

COME NOT to the Table without having your Hands and Face washed, and your Head combed.

Ask not for any Thing, but tarry until it be offered thee.

Find no fault with any Thing that is given thee.

If thou wantest any Thing from the Servants, call to them softly.

Make not a Noise with thy Tongue, Mouth, Lips, or Breath in eating or drinking.

Take not Salt with a greasy Knife.

Spit not, cough not, nor blow thy Nose at the Table, if it may be avoided; but if there be necessity, do it aside, and without much Noise.

Stuff not thy Mouth so as to fill thy Cheeks, be content with smaller Mouthfuls.

Blow not thy Meat, but with patience wait until it be cool.

Smell not of thy Meat, nor put it to thy Nose; turn it not the other Side upward to view it upon thy Plate.

Throw not any Thing under the Table.

Spit not forth any Thing that is not convenient to be swallowed, as the Stones of Plumbs, Cherries, or such like; but with thy left Hand, neatly move them to the Side of thy Plate.

Foul not the Napkin all over, but at one Corner only.

Stare not in the Face of any one, especially thy Superiours, at the Table.

Pick not thy Teeth at the Table, unless holding up thy Napkin before thy Mouth with thine other Hand.

Drink not nor speak with any Thing in thy Mouth.

When thou risest from the Table, having made a Bow at the Side of the Table where thou sattest, withdraw.

TABLE MANNERS
18th-century families could be as concerned about child-rearing as any are today, as witnessed by these rules for behavior at meals.

horse's bit. Slow learners found themselves wearing a tall pointed dunce's cap, seated in the corner on a stool. Trouble makers got a rap on the head with a ruler, perhaps a beating on the soles of their feet. When parents learned of a child's misbehavior, he often got another whipping at home—for being whipped at school.

Toys, both simple and elaborate, were imported from England. Indulgent and economical parents

THE IDEAL FAMILY In this group portrait of his own family, the painter John Singleton Copley contrasts the cool reserve of the men with the affection between women and children. Copley appears in the group behind his father. The child's rattle, similar to the one at left of silver and coral, attests to the family's wealth.

might also make them. Girls played with dolls and doll furniture, miniature animals and tea sets. A boy's most prized possession was a jackknife, with which he could whittle his own treasures, including bows and arrows, willow whistles, and tops for spinning. If the family did not have a dog or cat, children might make pets of wild fawns, squirrels, or raccoons.

Both boys and girls played endless variations of tag and hide-and-seek, as well as blindman's buff, hop-scotch, leapfrog, hoop-rolling, and other diversions called base-ball, trap-ball, stool-ball, hop-hat, tip-cat, shuttlecock, thread-the-needle, and I-sent-a-letter-to-my-love. Games especially favored by boys included marbles, top-whipping, and chuck-farthing, a game of skill in which coins were tossed into a hole.

In summer, children enjoyed swimming and fish-

ing; in winter, they took to local ponds with ice skates and to snow-covered hills with homemade wooden sleds. Children of wealthy parents learned minuets, country dances, and deportment from dancing masters. The highlights of a rural childhood were country fairs, with ox-pulling contests for the farmers, hearty family picnics, and boisterous games.

MUSIC LESSON Artist Lewis Miller captures the pleasure and pandemonium of a music lesson in a scene based on the German Lutheran school where his father taught. The list names boys and girls who were in the class. At right above, colonial boys play badminton in a woodcut from a 1787 book.

GREAT PLANTATIONS

Wealthy Southerners led lives of luxury in self-sufficient worlds of their own,

which they built on slave labor and profitable export crops. Socializing was predominantly

done at home, and often in exhaustingly high style.

THOUGH MOST PEOPLE in the South, like the North, were small farmers, the region in the 1700's became dominated by large plantations built on the export of tobacco, indigo, and rice. Compared with the average farm, they presented a striking picture indeed.

Most of the early plantations were owned—and ruled—not by titled Englishmen but by immigrants of modest origins who had risen to wealth and power through their own efforts, including shrewd trading and speculation in land. Warming to their new roles as country squires, these self-made men usually enjoyed a lifestyle equivalent to the minor gentry in England.

Some plantations were merely big. On the Potomac, George Mason looked out over 5,000 acres at Gunston Hall; his neighbor at Mount Vernon, George Washington, counted 8,000 acres. A few of the landholdings were immense. William Byrd, proprietor of Westover, a splendid Georgian mansion on the James River, owned nearly 180,000 acres in Virginia and Maryland. Robert ("King") Carter, whose descendants presided over Nomini Hall and Carter's Grove, had amassed more than 300,000 acres and 1,000 slaves by the time he died in 1732.

A successful planter usually acquired his land along a navigable river like the Potomac, the Rappahannock, or the James, where he could ship his crop from his own docks. In a parklike setting overlooking the river, he built his substantial brick house adapted from English models, complete with formal boxwood gardens. Some owners, with the help of gifted craftsmen—such as William Buckland, brought from England by George Mason—produced stately architecture and well-crafted interiors echoing the taste displayed in London homes.

To the sides and in back of the main house were various outbuildings, which

JEWEL ON THE POTOMAC Gunston Hall, George Mason's Georgian-style house, has been restored to 18th-century perfection, as have its formal gardens and deer park. The waters of Gunston Cove flow into the Potomac River.

RIDING TO HOUNDS Southern plantation owners attempted to recreate a society like that of the English landowners in their rustic surroundings, as shown in this painting of a Virginia fox hunt.

Within such worlds of their own, the "first families" of Virginia, Maryland, and the Carolinas lived lives of legendary luxury and ease. Surrounded by furnishings from England, or the fine pieces produced by colonial cabinetmakers as the century went on, they ate and drank from the finest imported china and glassware; a fancy dinner often ran to three separate courses of heavy foods, punctuated by toasts with a variety of wines. On special occasions they staged fish feasts, oyster roasts, and barbecues, or danced minuets and country dances at formal balls. Major events such as weddings and christenings were celebrated with house parties that sometimes went on for days.

might include a stable, coach house, henhouse, "necessary" (privy), dairy, granary, and a smokehouse for curing hams. A separate kitchen and laundry building, sometimes linked to the mansion by a covered breezeway, kept heat and cooking odors away from the house, and reduced the danger of fires to the main dwelling. Nearby were a large vegetable garden to supply the needs of family and guests, pasture land for the horses, and an orchard to provide apples, peaches, plums, persimmons, and pears. More discreetly removed were utilitarian quarters for the plantation's laborers, who worked in the fields or around the house. Somewhere in view of the fields was the plantation office, where the owner ran the affairs of the estate.

When not supervising their estates or balancing their books, the men raced horses, rode to hounds, hunted deer, hare, wild turkey, and other game (including buffalo, which in the 1700's could still be found in the valley of Virginia to the west). The women managed their households, planned menus, instructed servants, welcomed guests, and found time to do sewing and elaborate needlework. But many could, and did, ride a horse as well as a man.

There were few towns of consequence with the exception of Williamsburg, the colony's capital from

COPYBOOK CARPENTRY

A FINE PLANE This carpenter's tool was an object of beauty in itself.

LIKE OTHER COLONIAL MEN of high standing, George Mason probably drew up the floor plan and exterior for his new home, but he needed a skillful carpenter-builder to construct the woodwork he desired through-out the interior, in the Georgian stylethen fashionable in England. In London Mason's brother signed William Buckland, an English carpenter-joiner, to a four-year term of indenture in America to provide the woodwork for Gunston Hall.

In Buckland's luggage when he reached the colonies would have been at least one or two carpenter's handbooks. These practical guides to the design of such details as doorways, mantels, cornices, and windows, were widely used in the 18th century by artisans who adapted the designs to their own use. The books helped to spread English architectural styles throughout the colonies.

BY THE BOOK A staircase design from *The British Architect*, re-published in Philadelphia in 1775.

1699–1779. Virginians flocked to Williamsburg for the social life while the colonial assembly, the House of Burgesses, was in session.

Most of the time, however, planters and their families had to find their pleasures in their own, or other people's, homes. They

CHINESE EXPORT Porcelain from China, hand-painted with the family crest, was popular among the wealthy.

thought nothing of riding, coaching, or boating great distances to visit relatives or friends, and often stayed several days or weeks. Some isolated plantation owners were so hungry for company and news that they posted servants along nearby roads or rivers, with instructions to hail likely-looking travelers and invite them in for a good meal and a bed. George Washington had so many visitors that he described Mount Vernon as a "well resorted tavern," adding that it was populated by "people of the first distinction." He also complained that his guests were eating and drinking him into oblivion. Thus he revealed another side of Southern hospitality,

which—along with a general tendency to improvidence and living on credit—contributed to more than one plantation owner's downfall.

Most scions of the new aristocracy were well-educated by the standards of their time, and most were involved in government on the county or the colony level. Lower schools were slow in forming in the South, and the planters sent their children to a nearby minister, or to England, for education, or hired young men as tutors to teach English, Latin, arithmetic, philosophy, and a smattering of music and art.

Prosperous planters had time for politics, and many became active in resisting what they saw as unfair treatment of the colonies by England. Notably, four of the new country's first five presidents were Virginians.

DINNER: A GROANING BOARD

WHEN AN 18TH-CENTURY hostess set out a meal for guests, she arranged her serving dishes symmetrically to cover most of the table. A fork and knife would be set to the left and right of the plate as today. A folded napkin, into which a hard roll was often tucked, was placed on

top of the dinner plate. Dinner, the main meal of the day, began at 2 or 3 p.m. and often lasted for several hours, after which the ladies adjourned to the parlor to drink tea, and the men remained at the table drinking, smoking their pipes of tobacco, and offering toasts.

What is striking today is the richness and quantity of the food that was served at such a dinner. The chart above right, showing the placement of nine

WEIGHTY FARE An English engraving captures the mood of a lavish meal.

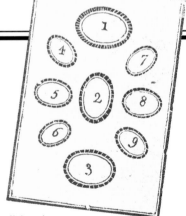

dishes, is accompanied by a suggested menu for two courses, the first of which includes the following fare: mackerel; herb soup; boiled goose and stewed red cabbage; breast of veal; chickens; lemon pudding; venison pasty; neck of venison; and mutton cutlets.

Suggestions for the second course are equally heavy.

SLAVE LIFE AND SLAVE LABOR

On the large tobacco, rice, and indigo plantations men, women, and

children as young as 13 often toiled in the fields from dawn to dark. In a land of free men

the slaves were bound to the land like human machines.

IN THE EARLY DAYS, plantation labor was supplied by indentured servants, young men and women from England who worked for a specified number of years in return for passage to the colonies and a promise of land. By the early 1700's, however, the flow of such voluntary immigrants had slowed, and was being replaced by an influx of black slaves.

The new arrivals, brought from Africa, were purchased by their owners for life, along with any offspring the women produced. Slaves had no contracts and no rights, though South Carolina decreed that they could not be forced to work more than 15 hours a day. A general attitude was expressed in 1749 by George Whitefield, a Methodist minister, who declared slaves "as necessary to the cultivation of Georgia as

axes, hoes, or any other utensils of agriculture."

The day of a typical plantation hand was described by an English observer, John Ferdinand Smyth:

"He is called up in the morning at daybreak, and is seldom allowed time enough to swallow three mouthfuls of hominy…but is driven out immediately to the field to hard labor, at which he continues, without intermission, until noon [when] he eats his dinner, and he is seldom allowed an hour for that….

"They then return to severe labor, which continues in the field until dusk…when they repair to the tobacco houses, where each has his task…allotted him. That employs him for some hours."

While field hands labored to bring in tobacco—the plantation's cash crop—life was only a little easier for

WOMEN WITH HOES Slave women who worked as field hands did the same backbreaking labor as the men. The job of the overseer was to be sure that the slaves did not slack in their work, and that they had no opportunity to rebel.

TO BE SOLD, on board the Ship *Bance-Island*, on tuesday the 6th of *May* next, at *Ashley-Ferry*; a choice cargo of about 250 fine healthy NEGROES, just arrived from the Windward & Rice Coast. —The utmost care has already been taken, and shall be continued, to keep them free from the least danger of being infected with the SMALL-POX, no boat having been on board, and all other communication with people from *Charles-Town* prevented.

Austin, Laurens, & Appleby.

N. B. Full one Half of the above Negroes have had the SMALL-POX in their own Country.

TRAGIC CARGO Slave sales were common in southern port cities. An outbreak of smallpox aboard a slave ship would cause the spread of alarm in any town where the ship docked.

83

RICE HOOK AND SCALE
Rice was the boom crop that brought plantation society to South Carolina. Slaves bent in shallow waters to cut the sheafs of the grain with short-handled rice hooks. The rice was pounded from the husks in hollowed-out logs and measured in a scale.

house slaves—the cooks who prepared meals, the waiters who served them, the maids who cleaned up and made beds, the gardeners who tended the gardens and grounds. Families sometimes felt genuine affection for slaves who had served the family for years.

Many owners were proud of their "people," as they called them, but left no question as to who was boss. Reprimands were delivered forcefully; more violent punishments were sometimes delegated to a hired overseer. Lagging on the job, insubordination, petty thievery, and leaving the plantation without permission were punished by whippings, the number of lashes determined by the severity of the offense. More heinous crimes—stealing from a master, assaulting a white person—usually meant death.

Except for a few favored servants like nurses, who slept in the main house near the children, slaves and their families lived in lofts, barracks, or rows of cabins, which were meagerly furnished. Meals consisted of corn, beans, and rice, with fish, pork, or other meat sometimes available. Slaves were encouraged to tend small vegetable gardens to supply their own food.

While house servants might be given presentable clothing, field hands wore garments of coarse fabric, often cut and sewn by a slave who served as the plantation's seamstress. Children went with little or no clothing at all. One traveler to Williamsburg noted: "I have seen boys of 10 and 12 years of age going through the streets quite naked, and others with only part of a shirt hanging part of the way down their backs. This is so common a sight that even the ladies do not appear to be shocked...."

HARVEST TIME
Branches of indigo are cut in August, when the plant is about five feet high and in bloom.

INDIGO BONANZA   South Carolina's second boom crop was indigo, thanks largely to one young girl who ran her father's plantation while he was away. In 1739 16-year-old Eliza Lucas began the successful cultivation of the plant, which produced a vivid blue dye used for coloring cloth. Processing required the plant's leaves to ferment, and was extremely smelly, but the dyes proved equal to those bought by the English from the West Indies. Planters took up the crop, along with rice, since indigo required higher ground, and 303,531 pounds of the dye were exported in 1755. The industry ended when the British stopped buying because of the Revolution.

SOAKING PROCESS
Plants soak for 12 hours or more in cypress vats. Water from the nearest river branch or stream is drawn into the vat by means of a wooden suction pump.

INDIGO MUD   The liquid is drained into an aerating vat, where it is stirred to a dark blue froth with "bottomless buckets" attached to poles. Lime water is added, precipitating a residue called Indigo Mud.

MUD INTO BRICKS
The mud is scraped from the vat into brick molds. Dried indigo "bricks" are loaded into barrels for shipping.

WEST TO THE WILDERNESS

Pioneers in Kentucky territory had to live close to the land—hunting, farming,

building their cabins with the help of neighbors, fashioning their own furniture and clothes.

And life on the frontier was always shadowed by the fear of Indian attack.

AS CHEAP LAND became scarce along the Eastern seaboard, more and more settlers headed westward for the Appalachian foothills and beyond to make their homes. Their mood was summed up later by the legendary wilderness scout Daniel Boone: "Too many people! Too crowded! I want more elbow room!"

The goal of many settlers was the territory known as Kentucky or "Kaintuck"—from the Cherokee name Ken-ta-ke ("great meadow")—a hunter's paradise where, it was said, the buffalo were so big that the meadows sank beneath their weight and the wild turkeys were so numerous they could not all fly at once. "Nature was here a series of wonders and a fund of delight," said Boone of an earlier exploration, and he was determined to bring his own wife and children to settle there.

In 1775, Boone helped the newly formed Transylvania Land Company claim a vast tract of land in the fertile bluegrass region south of present-day Lexington. To open it to settlement, he led 30 mounted woodsmen through the Appalachian Mountains at Cumberland Gap in southwestern Virginia. Laboring with axes, they improved ancient Indian trails and buffalo paths into what would become known as Wilderness Road, a gateway to the West through which some 300,000 settlers passed in the next 25 years. At Boonesborough, a small, fortified village they built at a terminus of the trail near the Kentucky River, the pioneers and their families soon found themselves under Indian attack. In 1776 Boone—who had lost one son in an earlier skirmish and was to lose another—barely rescued his daughter from capture by the Shawnee, and spent four months himself as the captive of a Shawnee tribe before escaping to defend his town in a nine-day siege in 1778.

Although an increasing number of settlements were harassed by hostile warriors—1777 was referred to as "the year of the bloody sevens"—immigrants continued to pour in. Many were of Scotch-Irish descent, from western Pennsylvania and the upcountry of Virginia, people noted for their toughness, independence, and willingness to fight. Virginia veterans of the American Revolution received bounties of land in

CUMBERLAND TRAIL Buffalo and deer had worn a path through this natural pass in the Allegheny Mountains long before people took up its use. Part of a "warrior's path" stretching from the Ohio to the Potomac, it was used by Indians for purposes of trade as well as for war. Many roads of the 18th century had similar origins.

the southwestern region of Kentucky.

Much of Wilderness Road was too narrow and rocky to accommodate wagons, so the first settlers traveled on horse or foot with as many other settlers as they could find to share the dangers of the trail. A typical young family was led by the husband, who walked ahead with his rifle ready in the crook of his arm. On a horse behind him rode his wife, and baby, if she had one, and as much as she could carry strapped to her saddle. On a lead rein behind her plodded a packhorse or mule loaded with precious possessions: a woodsman's axe, a farmer's hoe, and other vital tools; an iron pot and skillet for cooking; blankets and extra clothing; and sacks of corn to eat and plant as seed for a first crop. If the family owned a milk cow, she followed on a lead behind the packhorse, carrying a share of the burden, too.

SETTLING IN ON THE FRONTIER

When the couple arrived at a place that they hoped to settle, they staked out a claim near a creek or spring, marking its boundaries by chopping blazes in the bark of "witness trees" (also called "tomahawk claims"). For immediate shelter, they rigged a piece of canvas on poles or built a simple log lean-to, open to a cooking fire on one side, for temporary shelter.

To provide food, the husband hunted for deer, wild turkey, and geese, or settled for small game such as squirrels, woodchucks, and passenger pigeons. On the hunt, probably alone, he kept a wary eye out for Indians, and for rattlesnakes, wolves, "painters" (panthers), and black bears. If need be, he would shoot these, too.

Rattlesnake or panther meat made a welcome meal for more than one hungry settler, though for many it remained an acquired taste. Bear

BUCKSKINS Back country settlers ("buckskins") used rifles and powder horns for protection and hunting.

meat and grease were prized staples, and the pelts furnished warm bed coverings, coats, and rugs, though a large she-bear could be a formidable adversary, particularly if disturbed when she was with her cubs. Wolves were not regarded as useful game but as a menace to children and livestock. They were shot on sight, or caught in baited pits and traps.

Much of a settler's time was spent wielding an ax, to clear a patch of forest for farming and to provide wood for warmth, cooking, and building. A strong axman working alone could handle trees up to a foot thick. Larger trees that were in the way were simply girdled with a cut around the trunk and left to die; after a year or two a farmer might burn them where they stood, but he still had to hoe or plow around the stumps and roots to plant his crops.

As almost everywhere else in the colonies, corn was a key to

GETTING THERE

An early pioneer like this one wrote about a day of rugged journey with his mule through mountainous terrain: "Travel this day along a verey Bad hilley way." A detour of several hundred miles by river could be faster travel than getting to some places directly by foot, and a wagon was sometimes more hindrance than help. In rough country explorers might be happy to cover ten miles in a day.

survival in Kentucky and in the nearby territory that would become Tennessee. While a family might subsist on some of the precious kernels they had brought with them, they planted most of them between the stumps in their clearing, along with the seeds of beans, turnips, melons, pumpkins, and other vegetables that would supply fresh food.

FRONTIER SOCIAL LIFE

When their first harvest came in, new settlers eagerly gathered the ears and shucked them around the fire. In a later year, a larger harvest might provide an excuse for a corn-husking bee, to which a family invited other settlers, even if they lived miles away. The ears were heaped in two piles divided by a rail, and two teams were chosen up. At a given signal, each team dug into its pile and shucked away furiously, until someone shouted that his side had finished first. After much drinking and joking, everyone gathered for a hearty supper—which, of course, included corn.

An even bigger social event on the Western frontier

EDEN OF THE WEST

Kentucky, the 15th state in the Union, was the 18th-century promised land for Americans seeking homesites. Daniel Boone told of its "myriads of trees, some gay with blossoms, others rich with fruit," and of its fertile soil. Despite the rigors of frontier life, Kentucky had 74,000 inhabitants by 1790, the time of the first census.

was a house-raising, in which neighbors helped a new family get out of its temporary shelter and into a more substantial home. On the appointed day, guests arrived with their axes and some food; their host was expected to lay in an ample supply of homemade whiskey and venison or other fresh meat.

Most of the first day was spent felling and cutting trees into lengths for a structure generally about 20 feet long and 16 feet wide; additional logs were split into long boards that would be overlapped like shingles to cover the roof. Another day might be needed to

THE ENDLESS WORK OF SPINNING

WHEN A FRONTIER WOMAN'S other routine chores were done, she would turn to her spinning and weaving. It took great quantities of yarn to weave into the cloth needed for her family's clothing. If the family had sheep, she could spin wool, but more often she spun flax into linen. Flax was easy to grow—it could be planted in May and harvested before the end of June—but flax fibers are

tough and had to be soaked, pounded from the stalks, scraped, and broken down through several stages before the fibers were ready to be spun. From growing the flax to sewing the woven linen into a man's shirt could take as long as a year and a half.

Flax and wool required different spinning wheels. Both used the motion of the large wheel to wind the fibers onto a spindle, but the flax wheel was smaller, with a frame above the wheel for holding the flax fibers. The spinner sat alongside the wheel, fed the flax onto the bobbin, and pumped the treadle with her foot, replacing the bobbin when it

Flax spinning wheel

became full.

Linen was made into clothing and bedsheets; wool was woven into heavier clothes and blankets. When the two fibers were combined they became linsey-woolsey, a weft of warm wool woven onto a warp of tough linen threads. This was the fabric most in use on the frontier.

Woven wool coverlet

roll the big logs up inclined poles and notch them into place to form the walls, which were chinked with slivers of wood and a weathertight stuffing of moss mixed with mud.

A third day might be required to finish the roof, a floor for a loft, and a chimney of mud-plastered logs, which was placed slightly away from the walls to reduce the hazard of fire. Among the final tasks was installing a heavy plank door, which would be secured with a large cross-bar at night against surprise visitors. For the sake of safety, windows were kept to a minimum. The openings were made without glass, but with stout wooden shutters that could be closed during bad weather or an Indian attack. When the work was completed, everyone celebrated at a final supper until the time came for the guests to depart, leaving the owners to enjoy their new home.

Inside a typical frontier cabin, life was snug if spare. The floor was usually packed dirt, though some homes had a flooring of rounded half-logs, called puncheons, which were installed flat-side-up. More puncheons, with legs fitted into holes on their undersides, served as tables and benches, though some occupants might sit on nothing more than a "block cheer"—a short, heavy section of log upended and used as a stool. Beds and cradles were homemade, softened only slightly with rough mattresses or pads; bowls, trenchers, spoons, barrels, and pails were also made of wood. Meals were cooked in the open fireplace that served to heat the room. Unless the residents could make tallow candles or smoky, grease-burning lamps, the fire was also the only source of light at night.

BOONESBOROUGH   This outpost was built by Daniel Boone in 1775 as a refuge from hostile Indians and a stopover for settlers headed deeper into Kentucky. In 1778 it withstood a nine-day siege by Shawnee warriors.

BRINGING HOME THE BACON

A family made the most of what it had, including food. Corn and other grains were pounded into meal in a hollowed-out block, or ground into flour between flat, circular stones laboriously turned by hand. Corn went into everything, including mush, hominy grits, hoe-cake, and "johnnycake" (a dry, durable biscuit suitable for travelers that was originally called journeycake).

Almost every settler depended on owning a number of domestic pigs, which ran loose outside the cabin and foraged in the woods for nuts and roots. Many became so wild that "bringing home the bacon" often meant taking a rifle along. A hearty breakfast consisted of home-cured bacon or pork sausage in gravy, accompanied by fresh eggs, chicken, hot cornbread with butter and honey, coffee, and perhaps a dash of whiskey to ward off the chill. At dinner, pork, venison, tongue, squirrel, and pigeon, along with a crusty dough, went

A FRONTIER HOUSE-RAISING: MANY HELPING HANDS

The neighborliness with which rural Americans treated new arrivals is described in this account of an 18th-century house-raising on the frontier. The author, Hector St. John de Crèvecoeur, a French aristocrat-turned-farmer, had befriended the beneficiary, Andrew, a young Scottish immigrant.

❝I told him that the time had come to build his house; and that for the purpose I would myself invite the neighborhood to a frolic; that thus he would have a large dwelling erected, and some upland cleared, in one day. Mr. P. R., his old friend, came at the time appointed, with all his hands, and brought victuals in plenty; I did the same. About 40 people repaired to the spot; the songs, and merry stories, went round the woods from cluster to cluster, as the people had gathered to their different works; trees fell on all sides, bushes were cut up and heaped; and while many were thus employed, others with their teams hauled the big logs to the spot which Andrew had pitched upon for the erection of his new dwelling. We all dined in the woods; in the afternoon the logs were placed with skids, and the usual contrivances: thus the rude house was raised, and above two acres of land cut up, cleared, and heaped...Andrew was absolutely incapable of working; it was to him the most solemn holiday he had ever seen...he went from one to the other with the bottle in his hand, pressing everybody to drink, and drinking himself...[The house] was nothing more than a square inclosure, composed of 24 large clumsy logs, let in at the ends...

When the work was finished, the company made the woods resound with the noise of their three cheers, and the honest wishes they formed for Andrew's prosperity. He could say nothing, but with thankful tears he shook hands with them all.❞

A DAY'S WORK   A field could be cleared and a cabin could be built in a day with the help of neighbors.

into a variety of "pot pies," which resembled dumpling or meat-and-vegetable stews. A good pie was soft and tender enough to be eaten with a spoon; if there were any leftovers, which rarely happened, they were easily put aside, supplemented with other ingredients, and reheated for another meal. Some meat was saved and preserved for future use by smoking it or pickling it in brine, or by cutting slabs into thin strips and drying them as "jerky," a handy source of protein that sustained many a pioneer while out on the trail.

Meals were usually washed down with milk from the family cow, which also provided the family with buttermilk, butter, and cheese. In households that had their own crude stills—and there were many—a popular drink was the raw, potent whiskey known as "corn likker" (it was not until later that the famous, and more palatable, Kentucky bourbon was first distilled).

When a settler had managed to get an orchard going, a portion of the harvest of apples or other fruits would go into making his own cider or brandy.

WHAT THE PIONEERS WORE

The first settlers had to make and mend most of their own clothes, which they fashioned by tanning leather from animal skins, spinning wool from sheep, or weaving linen from the flax they grew in their fields. While men often wore homemade fur hats in winter, they were not necessarily of the famous coonskin type. In summer a more practical choice was an ordinary farmer's hat, plaited from straw or reeds.

Almost no one wore the fringed jackets of buckskin associated with the frontier, except perhaps to social gatherings. Leather was notorious for being cold and clammy when it got wet—though many men adopted the buckskin leggings worn by many Indians because they were durable and resisted scratches from the underbrush. A more common upper garment was a hunting shirt, a long, loose tunic made of coarse linen or a warmer woolen blend called linsey-woolsey. It was made without buttons, but simply overlapped in front and was held closed at the waist with a belt, from which hung a long-bladed hunting knife and perhaps a tomahawk.

Women's clothes consisted of linen shifts or smocks, neckerchiefs, and limp-brimmed sunbonnets tied under the chin, supplemented in cooler weather with a shawl and perhaps a lumpy fur hat. Both men and women wore Indian-style moccasins, hunters preferring ones with high, protective cuffs like those of boots. These, too, were uncomfortable when wet, had to be stuffed with leaves or hair to make them tolerably warm, and required frequent patching and resewing after long days of use.

Children in early Kentucky wore much the same clothes as their parents, and shared the same life, fetching firewood and water, bringing in the cow for milking and helping in the fields. Toys were scarce, although a girl might have a cornhusk doll, which settlers learned from the Indians how to make; games were made up. Education was largely nonexistent, restricted to the teachings of mothers or fathers who were often illiterate themselves. Children were taught practical skills at an early age: girls learned cooking, sewing, and weaving; boys learned how to hunt, trap, fish, and survive in the woods. A boy might learn marksmanship by practicing at first with a bow and arrow. At the age of 12 or 13, he progressed to shooting his father's long rifle, or best of all, one of his own. The gun was no toy, but a deadly weapon that could pierce the heart of a fleeing deer—or an oncoming Indian—at a range of 200 yards. One never knew when it might be needed to provide for, or defend, the family, and, later, a family of one's own.

The ambition of every frontier boy was to become as accurate as the marksmen who competed at local shooting matches, which were often held in connection with weddings and other events. The target was usually sim-

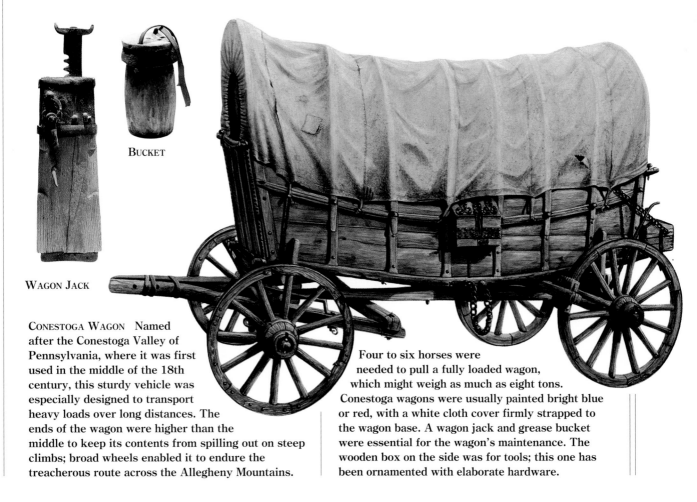

BUCKET

WAGON JACK

CONESTOGA WAGON Named after the Conestoga Valley of Pennsylvania, where it was first used in the middle of the 18th century, this sturdy vehicle was especially designed to transport heavy loads over long distances. The ends of the wagon were higher than the middle to keep its contents from spilling out on steep climbs; broad wheels enabled it to endure the treacherous route across the Allegheny Mountains.

Four to six horses were needed to pull a fully loaded wagon, which might weigh as much as eight tons. Conestoga wagons were usually painted bright blue or red, with a white cloth cover firmly strapped to the wagon base. A wagon jack and grease bucket were essential for the wagon's maintenance. The wooden box on the side was for tools; this one has been ornamented with elaborate hardware.

RARE HIGHWAY In the late 1700's most roads lacked surface, grading, or drainage, and were turned into quagmires by heavy rain. Benjamin Latrobe's sketch of a divided New Jersey road belies typical conditions.

ple, and impossibly difficult to a casual observer's eye: the head of a handwrought iron nail pounded into a board. The audience wasn't talking about carpentry when they said the winner "hit the nail on the head."

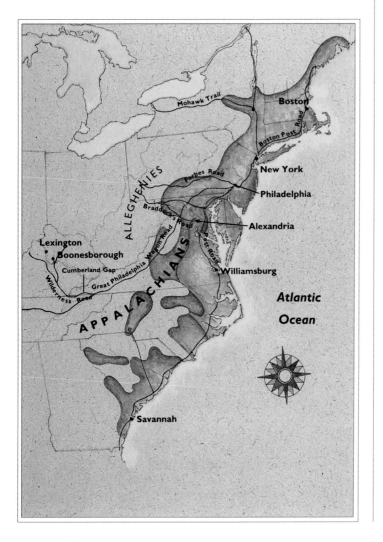

CLAIMING THE NEW LAND

To legally acquire a homesite in Kentucky, a Virginia county until 1792, settlers usually had to purchase the land from speculators who had preceded them. Prices were so high that even wealthy planters held no more than a few hundred acres. Many settlers remained landless tenants or settled in poorer areas surrounding the prime bluegrass lands.

The settler—or land speculator—first had to secure a warrant from Virginia. The next step was to hire a surveyor, who would measure the claim, establish the property lines, and register it in the name of the new owner.

One of the leading surveyors was the indomitable Daniel Boone, who sometimes claimed land for his customers that had already been registered to others. It is said that Boone also sometimes put off registering the land he had surveyed while he went hunting. Boone was deluged by law suits and was driven into poverty. He blamed much of his problem on legalistic New Englanders, saying he preferred not to live "within 100 miles of a damned Yankee."

Boone represented Kentucky twice in the Virginia General Assembly, in 1781 and 1791. Always seeking more open space for himself and his family, he later moved on to Missouri, where he lived until 1821.

MAIN ROADS AND CROPS Midway through the 18th century a post road existed from Maine to Savannah. Other roads had evolved from Indian trails and two bore the names of the generals who had them built to move troops during the French and Indian War. Most settlers lived in one of three farming regions, indicated by their main crops of rice and indigo (blue), tobacco (tan), and cattle and grain (red).

Sea Trade and City Life

THE TONTINE COFFEE HOUSE, NEW YORK CITY

American culture and industry were born in the colonial port cities.

Craftsmen provided products and services as they created new American styles,

and trader-merchants raised entrepreneurial skills to new heights.

When not working, city dwellers enjoyed a full social life: the men flocked to taverns,

while women enjoyed afternoon teas at home with friends.

But urban life could be perilous—rampaging fires, poor sanitation, epidemics

of infectious diseases, and crime were also part of everyday life in colonial cities.

GREAT PORTS, TALL SHIPS

The vibrant centers of commerce and culture in 18th-century America were its major port

cities—Boston, Newport, New York, Philadelphia, and Charleston—through whose bustling

streets and warehouses poured a flood of immigrants and goods of every kind.

PHILADELPHIA, the largest colonial city, was a hotbed of activity—a greater variety of crafts flourished and more goods were made there than in any other colonial town. One traveler from England observed that the city's artisans had "made great advances in most of the British manufactures here...hardware, clocks, watches, locks, guns,

flints, glass, stoneware, nails, paper, cordage, cloth, etc." The city was known for its silversmiths and cabinetmakers, whose fine work was widely in demand.

Nowhere was the collaboration between urban craftsmen and merchants more productive than in the prime industry of Philadelphia and its sister ports: shipbuilding. By the mid-1700's, the larger cities

THRIVING WATERFRONT An oceangoing merchant ship is docked near a smaller trading vessel at Philadelphia's busy Arch Street Ferry, one of the city's centers for trade. Near the waterfront was Elfreth's Alley (inset), where shipwrights, boatbuilders, blacksmiths, ship captains, and other residents who drew their livelihood from the sea occupied the small houses. Built between 1713 and 1811, the houses are still occupied today.

could draw on a broad range of talented artisans, called "mechanicks," as well as a bountiful supply of oak, pine, and other trees ideal for maritime use.

With such assets—and the ingenuity for which Americans were becoming famous—colonial shipyards were able to produce superior sailing vessels, not only for colonial merchants but for English owners, who found they could have ships built more efficiently and cheaply in the colonies than at home. Even the Royal Navy—which tried with mixed success to reserve for itself the colonies' finest tall white pine trees for use as masts—admitted admiration for the way American ships were built.

Each year American shipwrights turned out hundreds of sloops and schooners for local fishing fleets, and for merchants trading up and down the coast. These ships also transported much of the colonies' passengers and mail because of the scarcity of decent roads.

The builders' greatest efforts, however, were reserved for the great, square-rigged "topsail ships" destined for ports in Europe and the Orient. Building such a large vessel took close to a year, requiring a great deal of organization and the skills of as many as 30 trades. Indeed, the building of wooden ships has been described as the supreme achievement of early American craftsmanship.

BUILDING A SHIP

The shell of the vessel, the hull, was laid out by master shipwrights, sea-wise carpenters who first developed small-scale models and then full-sized templates for key parts, often selecting the timbers themselves.

With broad axes and adzes, carpenters cut and fitted pieces together to form the ship's keel, forward stem, and stern post, assembling them on a foundation of squared timbers resembling railroad ties that sloped down from the shipyard to the water's edge. Next they fashioned the U-shaped ribs for the hull, tilt-

SHIPYARD WORK A frigate is under construction at Southwark, one of Philadelphia's busiest shipyards, where men-of-war and merchant ships were turned out. The skills of a ship's carpenter surpassed those of his landsman brother, since his workmanship had to prove seaworthy.

ed them up into place, and fastened them closely together along the keel. Lastly, they enclosed the frames with planking, inside and out, and with decking on top. The boards were cut by sawyers working in a sawpit, one man above and another down below—the latter sputtering in a constant shower of sawdust—alternately pulling and pushing a long, two-man saw. The carpenters carefully fitted the boards together and secured them with treenails (pronounced "trunnels"), stout wooden pegs that were pounded into bored holes.

While the carpenters were finishing their work, caulkers were busy making the hull and decking watertight. They stuffed the thousands of seams with oakum, a loose hemp fiber made by untwisting old ropes (a job often done by pensioners in old sailors' homes). Lengths of hemp were pressed into place by running a small wheel down each seam, then the hemp pounded tight with wedges and mallets and sealed with hot tar. To protect the wood against boring worms and barnacles, the bottom of the hull was coated with more tar, or a mixture of resin, sulfur, and tallow. For added durability, owners who could afford it had their vessels sheeted in copper plates. When the

95

MEN OF BUSINESS
Massachusetts merchants meet with an Englishman while wives look on in this 1790 painting on a tea tray. Costume and furnishings were so similar at the time, the interior could be American or English.

hull was finished, it was braced in a temporary cradle, resting on greased rails and held back by blocks, until time for the launching.

The lines for the rigging were made on the waterfront in long sheds called ropewalks. Professional ropers spun hemp into yarn, and twisted the yarn into varying thicknesses of line, including mainstays and anchor cables that might be many inches thick. The sails that would power the ship were fashioned by sailmakers, who cut and stitched their canvas in lofts large enough to lay a huge mainsail out on the floor.

Other craftsmen, meanwhile, made the hundreds of other items the ship would require. Blacksmiths forged anchors, chains, hinges, eyebolts, and the large iron bands that secured mast sections together. Blockmakers made dozens of metal-strapped wooden pulleys for handling the lines. Joiners built hatches, ladders, lockers, and furnishings. Painters finished trim and interiors. Ship chandlers supplied lamps, oil, and other ship's stores. Instrument makers provided compasses, chronometers, and sextants to keep the ship on course.

A major launching was a gala event. Often schools and shops would be closed so that everyone could turn out to watch the show. The ceremony would begin with the blessing of the vessel, gaily bedecked with flags, by a clergyman. Then the christening by the owner or a senior member of the crew would fol-

RICH CARGO Salem, Massachusetts, had become the nation's richest city per capita at the end of the 18th century, largely because of trade in Oriental luxuries brought into the port from halfway around the world aboard the great East Indiaman merchant ships. The painting above shows such a vessel, the *John*, being unloaded at a busy Salem wharf. A cargo that includes cinnamon, coffee, tea, pepper, and cloves scents the air as crew members off-load a bale of cotton and barrels of sugar. Because it is low tide, the stern of the *John* and its long-boat stand exposed in the harbor mud. On the wharf,

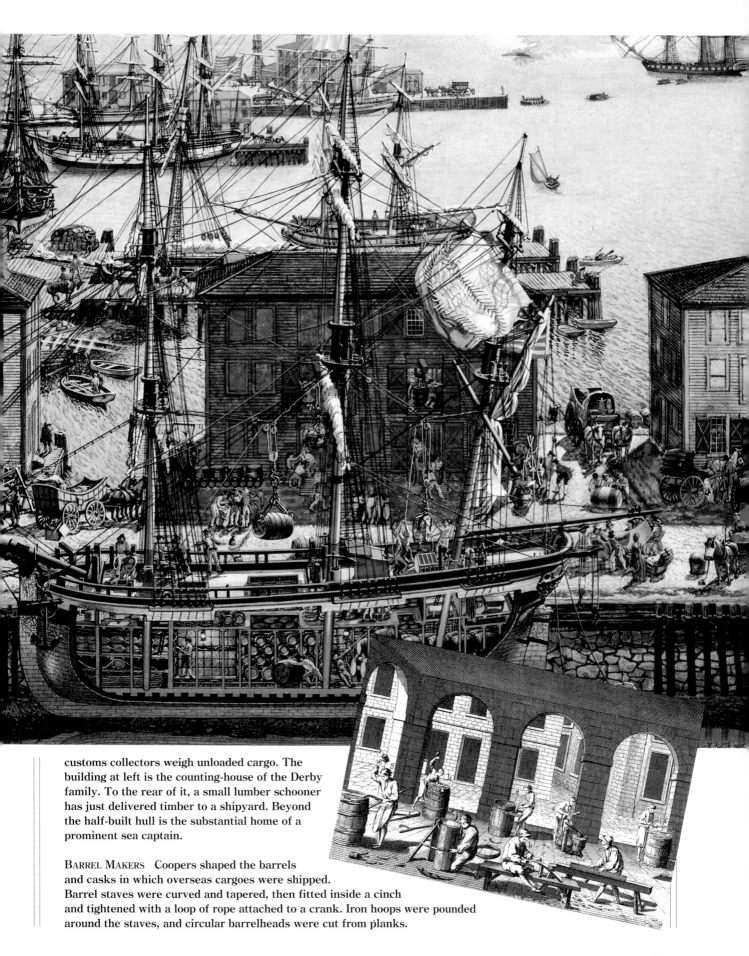

customs collectors weigh unloaded cargo. The
building at left is the counting-house of the Derby
family. To the rear of it, a small lumber schooner
has just delivered timber to a shipyard. Beyond
the half-built hull is the substantial home of a
prominent sea captain.

BARREL MAKERS   Coopers shaped the barrels
and casks in which overseas cargoes were shipped.
Barrel staves were curved and tapered, then fitted inside a cinch
and tightened with a loop of rope attached to a crank. Iron hoops were pounded
around the staves, and circular barrelheads were cut from planks.

ADVICE TO A CAPTAIN

❝You having the Command of the *Charming Lydia* Brigatine and She in all Respects fitt for the sea, My Order to you is that you take the first wind & weather for Sailing and proceed.... You have Invoice & Bill of Lading Inclosed Consigned yourself, you are to procure a Load of Molasses & proceed back to Boston & if you have more cargo than Loads you, then Ship it on the best Terms you Can in Molasses or bring it in Indigo.... See that your Casks be Good, & well Stow'd, bring me some fruit for the officers if any to be had, be prudent & saving of Expenses.... The Good Lord protect you & our Interests, from all Dangers & Enemies & Give you Conduct & prudence in all things to act for the Best, I wish you a Good Voyage & am your Owner.❞

Thomas Hancock to Captain Simon Gross, December 1743.

SEXTANT This instrument measured the angle of the sun above the horizon to help determine a ship's latitude.

---

low. As spectators watched breathlessly, the holding ropes were cut, the blocks were knocked out, and, with an ominous creaking, the hull began to slide toward the water. The grease on the rails smoked, and sometimes burst into flames from friction under the hull's considerable weight. On occasion, a ship might grind to an embarrassing halt—or, worse, tip over onto its side. But if all went well, it hit the water stern first with a splash, sending up a huge wave and a cheer from the crowd.

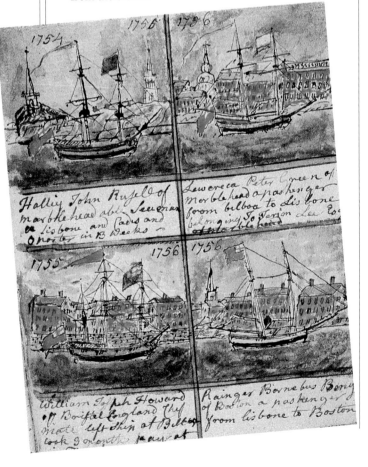

THE SAILOR'S LIFE

When the crew for a new ship was finally signed on, she raised her sails proudly and pulled away from the wharf to seek her fortunes at sea. Though there were usually a few old salts on board (including perhaps a disgruntled deserter or two from the British navy), most crew members were surprisingly young—the average age of a typical crew, including officers, was probably no more than 22.

Youth was a prerequisite since the sailor's life, by its very nature, demanded agility and a willingness to take risks. Also shipowners like Elias ("King") Derby, Salem's most famous merchant prince, liked to start discipline early by sending their heirs and relatives to sea when they were 15 or so to "learn the ropes," so that they could be put in charge of valuable cargoes. The merchantman *Benjamin*, which made one of the first successful voyages to the Pacific in 1792 to open up the East Indian trade, was commanded by a trio of "Derby's boys." The captain, Nathaniel Silsbee, was all of 19, his first mate, Charles Derby, was 20, and the ship's clerk, Richard Cleveland, was 18.

Even younger were the youths who made up the bulk of the crews, which totaled some 20 men on larger ships. Many were farm boys lured by tales of adventure and well-paid jobs, hoping that one day they might be sailing ships of their own.

A voyage to Europe—called downhill because the

CAPTAIN'S DIARY Watercolor sketches document ships encountered by Captain Ashley Bowen, of Marblehead, Massachusetts, whose lively career at sea began as a cabin boy and included hunting whales and fighting on a privateer.

prevailing winds were aft—took a month or more, and the return uphill could take three months; getting to the East Indies and back could take a year. For young apprentice seamen, much of this time was spent clambering up and down ratlines and edging out on spars to set, shorten, or strike the ship's multitude of sails— a dangerous task even in good weather, and one that could easily be fatal in a high wind or rain.

Between their four-hour turns on watch, crewmen lived below decks in the cramped, stuffy quarters of the forecastle, where the smells were frequently bad, the ship's motion was sickening, and a tall man could not stand up straight. They slept in hammocks or crude stacked bunks; ate hardtack, dried peas, salted meat, and occasionally fresh fish; and fought off bore-

dom by whittling, swapping stories, joining in rollicking sea chanteys with their mates, or playing cards.

Seasickness, homesickness, and other aspects of the sailor's life could take their toll. After only six days at sea, one miserable novice wrote in his diary: Monday, October 24—the day was stormy I wish I were home of all the places on earth there is no place like home I wanted to go to sea and now I have got enough of it Sunday I laid in my bunk and cried...."

CONVERSATIONS AT SEA During a period of strained relations between England and America, an English sea captain and the American master of the coastal vessel *Tabitha* hurled insults at each other through speaking trumpets, a moment witnessed and amusingly recorded by the artist Benjamin Latrobe. If a merchant ship was due to set sail without a full load, a ship's captain might advertise for passengers or small freight loads, as seen in this newspaper clipping. The benefits of a seagoing career are suggested by the painting of *Moses Marcey of Sturbridge*, (inset, top right), which includes a merchant's ship and the home of a prominent citizen. The subject, at leisure with his punch bowl, pipe, and accounts ledger, is probably a retired merchant or sea captain.

MERCHANTS AND ARTISANS

As tradesmen prospered, their standard of living rose, and this new wealth

was reflected in everything from architecture and furniture to household items and personal

belongings. Decorative arts flourished as city life took on elegance and sophistication.

BEHIND THE BUSTLING WATERFRONTS of America's port cities stood merchants and sea captains who were acute businessmen and risk-takers. One observer characterized them as "distinguished by a lively imagination.... Their enterprises are sudden, bold, and sometimes rash. A general spirit of adventure prevails...."

Some adventurers staked fortunes on a single voyage and came home penniless. Even established traders saw their businesses go sour. Recalled one New England shipowner who had been handsomely successful: "Then came a long series of disasters, ruinous voyages...bad management...I found myself bankrupt...reduced in a few years from affluence to complete destitution."

Many, however, profited from a steadily growing trade with England and Europe—or from any opportunity they saw. One was the infamous triangular trade, in which a merchant from Newport or Boston sent his ships to the West Indies for sugar and molasses, turned them into rum in his own distillery, took the rum to Africa's west coast to trade for slaves, carried the slaves back to the West Indies, and sold them to plantation owners—for sugar and molasses that could be made into more

CITYSCAPES This handsome row of 18th-century brick town houses on Market Street in Philadelphia, begun in 1786, was designed and built as rental property by Benjamin Franklin. One building housed the office of a newspaper published by Franklin's grandson. At left, a 1770 British broadside predicts a dynamic future for the city of Boston, shown as a place of ships and spires, "where ye inhabitants are industrious in every art to provide themselves with ye manufactures that Great Britain used to furnish them."

WITHDRAWING ROOM
Musical instruments
reflected Mr. Otis's gifts
as an amateur composer.

KITCHEN
The chimney
used for
cooking also
warmed the
bedroom
above. House
servants
lived on the
third floor.

PANTRY
Servants here
arranged food
passed from
the kitchen to
serve in the
dining room.

DINING ROOM
The wallpaper was vibrant
and the woodwork was painted
deep colors. Wall-to-wall
carpeting here and above was
a sign of luxurious living.

A BOSTON MANSION   Prosperous city residents made their homes places for entertaining. Harrison and Sally Otis
were a wealthy young couple who chose their friend Charles Bulfinch to design their Boston townhouse, built in
1795-96, in the Federal style of the day. Behind the formal facade, the dining room was the scene of many
fashionable dinners, attended by such notable guests as President John Quincy Adams. After dinner the men
climbed the stairs to the withdrawing room, the most opulent room in the house, for brandy and cigars, while
the women had tea in the formal ground-floor parlor. Bulfinch became one of the best-known architects in
America. The house is occupied today by the Society for the Preservation of New England Antiquities.

PORTRAIT PAINTING COMES OF AGE

IN THE COLONIES a would-be limner, or portrait painter, often had to support himself with practical jobs like varnishing, glazing, or silvering mirrors. A Maryland practitioner offered to paint "Altar Pieces for Churches, Land-scapes, Views of... Houses and Estates, Signs or any other way of Painting, and also Gilding." Even one of America's finest portrait painters, John Singleton Copley, complained of Bostonians' disregard for his craft: "The people generally regard it as no more than any other useful trade, as they sometimes term it, like that of a Carpenter or shew maker, not as one of the most noble Arts in the World."

Toward the end of the 18th century, the status of Copley and other painters markedly improved, as portraits became the rage among merchants and plantation owners who were willing to pay good money to have themselves and their families immortalized. An enterprising Englishman, John Wollaston, made a prosperous living painting the "faces" of nearly 300 aristocrats from Charleston to New York.

Charles Willson Peale, was the most versatile of the early American portraitists. He first learned saddlery as an apprentice in Annapolis, opened his own harness shop at the age of 20, added clock-making and repair to his services, and also did some sign painting

TRIM FIT
George Washington was 40 when Charles Willson Peale painted his portrait in the uniform of the Virginia State Militia he had worn years earlier as a young officer.

and silversmithing on the side. It was his talent for painting portraits, though, that attracted a group of local gentlemen, who offered to finance his further study in London. Peale pursued his new calling in Philadelphia, where he won considerable fame, painting his well-known portraits of George Washington, Benjamin Franklin, and John Paul Jones.

IN THE PICTURE
Tea is served under the approving gaze of their ancestors in this portrait by Johann Eckstein of a prominent family named Samels.

rum. Still other fortunes were made by enterprising New Englanders who went halfway around the world to trade for the treasures of the Orient, or to hunt for whales.

Those who succeeded celebrated their newfound status by surrounding themselves with elegant furniture, silver, crystal, and china. They dressed in the latest fashions from London and immortalized themselves by sitting for artists who painted their portraits, which they displayed on their parlor walls. For diversion they held lavish dinners and fancy balls, attended plays and concerts, and during the day were often seen "taking the air" in coaches driven by their servants through the streets.

But such ostentation did not sit well with everyone. In Philadelphia, a city of sober Quakers, a bit of doggerel titled "To Spring" summed up the general view:

Now the pleasant time approaches;
Gentlemen do ride in coaches.
But poor men they don't regard
That to maintain them labor hard.

HAIL AND FAREWELL Carpenter Henry Anhorn adorned his shop sign with symbols of the cradle-to-grave usefulness of his cabinetmaking skills.

"POOR MAN'S SILVER"
A cabinet of pewter at Winterthur Museum shows the remarkable versatility of the metal, which could be molded into everything from platters, porringers, and tankards to shoe buckles, buttons, and lamps. Much of the colonial pewterer's work consisted of melting down worn pieces and then remolding them in the current style.

THE FIRST UNIONS

Organized labor began in America when craftsmen formed associations to regulate their conduct and promote business. The first actual union was organized in Philadelphia in 1794, by journeymen shoemakers whose goals were higher wages, shorter hours, and improved working conditions. In 1799 the shoemakers managed to force their wages up after a nine-day strike, the first of its kind in the United States.

RISING ARTISANS

In the economic race, tradesmen often earned a respectable living; the ambitious did very well. The goods and services of shopkeepers and craftsmen were in demand in all cities, and not only by the rich. An ordinary consumer walking down a street in New York or Philadelphia could choose among a variety of specialized establishments, where competition not only stimulated new ideas but also tended to keep prices within bounds.

Since many of their customers were illiterate, artisans often embellished their shop fronts with colorful symbols of their trades: a wheelwright might display a brightly painted cart-wheel; a blacksmith, an oversize horseshoe; an optician, a large pair of eyeglasses; a dentist, a giant molar; a shoemaker, a large wooden boot; and a tailor, a big pair of shears.

As a small businessman, an artisan produced mostly according to "bespoke work," made to his customer's requests, though he might place some popular ready-made items on display. In cities his shop was usually on the ground floor of a modest urban house, with his kitchen in the cellar and his sleeping quarters on the second floor.

The workday was long, often starting at daybreak and continuing until dusk. A craftsman often was assisted by his wife, who greeted customers and kept the books, or a daughter who did chores, and a son who was learning his

father's trade. If the business warranted, he might employ a journeyman, a man who had completed an apprenticeship and now worked for wages.

More likely a master artisan relied on an apprentice, a boy placed with the craftsman to learn the trade. In return for his bed and board with the craftsman's family, the apprentice did the menial jobs of the craft while learning from his master, and was often taught how to read, write, and keep the business accounts as well. The

PHILADELPHIA'S BEST
The trade card of Benjamin Randolph suggests the highly rococo style of English Chippendale furniture that the cabinetmaker produced in his shop, opened in 1767. The ornately carved Chippendale side chair is one of his pieces.

apprentice was bound by the terms of his contract of indenture, generally four to seven years, or until he reached the age of 21. Upon completion of the contract the master was obliged to send him out into the world with a small stake ("freedom dues") that could include clothing, money, or a set of tools. Indentured apprentices were common in highly skilled trades like printing and silversmithing, but were also found in other crafts. Many distinguished Americans started under the apprentice system, including Benjamin Franklin, who began his career in a printer's shop.

Franklin and other printers were vital to the colonies' intellectual, political, and commercial development. They printed handbills, almanacs, journals, and books, as well as advertisements for other artisans' wares. As publishers of gazettes and newspapers, moreover, they also played leading roles in the exchange of information and ideas. They assumed an increasing leadership in public affairs—including the movement that eventually led to the American Revolution.

WILLIAMSBURG MILLINERY Hats, hoods, caps, turbans, and bonnets were all sold in this shop. Thick "pudding caps" like the one at left (probably made in England), were worn by toddlers to protect their heads if they fell.

Barbers and hairdressers not only cut hair but made and maintained wigs for well-to-do ladies and gentlemen. Many women skilled with a needle and thread hired themselves out as seamstresses in order to make ends meet. Some became successful enough to open their own dressmaking, millinery, or embroidery shops to serve the wealthy.

For those who could afford it, silverware was an excellent investment: a fancy bowl or an elaborate tea service was not only beautiful, and a mark of social status, but it was a convenient way to preserve wealth in salable form. Silversmiths like Paul Revere of Boston and Philip Syng of Philadelphia took their craft to new levels of art.

Colonial cabinetmakers or "joiners" such as Philadelphia's Benjamin Randolph were commissioned by leading families to create furniture of distinction for their homes, especially in the the graceful Queen Anne or ornate Chippendale style.

TIGHT LACING Fashion at mid-century required women to wear hair piled high and bodices that gave a cone-shaped silhouette. During the 1780's skirt hoops worn over false hips were replaced by artificial rumps, which became known as bustles.

THE RISE OF FASHION

STATUS IN THE COLONIES, as in Europe, was measured by the clothes one wore, and wealthy women wore the best they could afford to distinguish themselves from those whose clothing was merely practical. Fashion-conscious women imported the latest styles directly from England or France, or had copies made by skilled colonial tailors and seamstresses.

Fashionable women's clothing consisted of several layers beginning with a shift over which a bodice or boned corset (stays) and multiple petticoats were worn. Hoops tied around the waist under the gown held the skirts out. Shifts were long and loose, made of linen or cotton, and worn night and day. No underdrawers or pantaloons were worn under the skirts until the 19th century.

Fashion was not limited to clothing. Complicated hairstyles, such as the towering pompadour that originated in France, became popular and created a need for skilled hairdressers who used such things as straw, hay, horsehair, wool, old hair salvaged from used wigs, and even cow's tails to maintain the necessary elevation of these elaborate constructions. After such an investment of time and money, these fashionably coiffed women were reluctant to destroy their new look by brushing or washing their hair—which as a consequence was more likely to become infested with insects and other vermin than their lower-class counterparts whose hair was frequently brushed clean. Many found this unsanitary pretension silly; a Philadelphia Quaker, Elizabeth Drinker, wrote in her diary on July 4, 1778, "A very high head-dress was exhibited through the streets this afternoon on a very dirty woman, with a mob after her with drums, etc., by way of ridiculing that very foolish fashion."

Cosmetics were not so widely used in the colonies as in Europe. But the same women who styled their hair were likely to paint their skin. *The Toilet of Flora* was a popular book that discussed methods of preparing perfumes, powders, and "cosmetics of every kind, that can smooth and brighten the skin, give force to beauty, and take off the appearance of old age and decay."

PASTE JEWELRY A silver necklace of brilliants and mother-of-pearl is typical of the semi-precious jewelry imported from England in the mid-18th century.

Bathing was considered unhealthy, even dangerous. Colonial men and women washed in spots with lye soap, but rarely immersed themselves in water. Perfumes were used to mask their natural body odors.

Jewelry in many forms—pins, rings, necklaces, lockets, and fancy buttons made of enamel, paste, gilt, silver, or pearls and other gems—was widely available in the colonies after the middle of the 18th century. Silk stockings, fans, embroidered pocketbooks and umbrellas were other fashionable accessories used around this time.

FASHION DOLL Seamstresses dressed such dolls to show their skills. Under this fancy dress are undergarments the seamstress might copy.

STEPPING OUT Women's dress shoes were often made of damask and brocade. In the 18th century, shoes for left and right feet were identical.

HIGH HOSE Silk hose were worn by men or women; white ones were considered the most formal. Ribbon garters held them above the knee.

PLEASURES AND DIVERSIONS

Colonial cities offered an array of pastimes suited to every taste. For some, a welcome change

might be a simple outing in the countryside for fishing or a brief carriage ride.

Others looked to taverns or theaters for stimulation, or entertained friends at home.

BY THE MID-1700'S, taverns had grown into major centers of social life in city and country alike, especially for men. Establishments ranged from seedy grogshops near the waterfront, frequented by sailors and prostitutes, to elegant uptown inns and taprooms. Each had its regular customers, who could drop in of an afternoon or evening and be assured of conviviality among others of similar interests. They were places to acquire information—to talk to voyagers from other cities and countries, to read the latest newspaper, to consult the profusion of notices, advertisements, and messages posted on the walls. They were also important places of business: merchants and traders, as well as lawyers, government officials, and others often repaired to their favorite bars to work out deals.

Many taverns were the meeting grounds of private men's clubs—Masonic and other fraternal orders, "philosophical" societies, and groups who had banded together for the sole purpose of dining and drinking well, swapping stories, and enjoying themselves away from the prying eyes of wives. At such all-male gatherings, one might witness more than one loud argument, a brawling fist fight, and even a challenge to a duel. But conversation could also be serious, reaching high levels of science, literature, or the arts.

Often the subject was politics, includ-

ing discussions of the latest tax or other indignity imposed on the colonies by the British Crown. The American Revolution, it can be fairly said, began in the smoke-filled taverns of Boston and Williamsburg.

Taverns were popular places to drop in for a game of billiards, cards, shuffleboard, skittles, or dice—and to bet heavily on the results. To bring in customers, some pubs offered additional entertainment in the form of musicians, traveling shows, cockfights, or animal curiosities like a live camel or trained bear. Larger, more respectable inns had public rooms that could be rented for banquets and balls, in which ladies participated as enthusiastically as men.

Because some authorities regarded "tippling houses" as threatening to community morals, particularly in Puritan Boston and Quaker Philadelphia, they came under close regulation. In many places a tavern keeper was told what he could fairly charge for food, drink, and lodging—and how much liquor he was allowed to serve an individual, lest the customer should become "bereaved or disabled in the use of his understanding."

Such laws, of course, were not observed in

FANCY GAMES
Cards and betting were common even in the parlors of New England by the mid-18th century, when Mercy Otis Warren embroidered this elaborate tabletop for her home in Plymouth, Massachusetts.

DINNER SWEETS
An assortment of
"sweetmeats and
fruits" often followed
an elegant meal.
This table at
Winterthur Museum
holds a sampling
of iced almonds,
fruit-flavored sugar
drops, and
preserved apricots.

every case. Young John Adams noted in his diary that on any given evening one could find taverns "full of People, drinking Drams, Phlip, Toddy, Carrousing, Swearing," and, wryly, that "here diseases, vicious habits, bastards and legislators are frequently begotten." Neglecting to mention how he did his extensive research, he solemnly declared: "Let others waste the bloom of Life, at the Card or billiard Table, among rakes and fools."

More genteel diversions were favored by the upper classes. Among women of leisure, "taking tea" in each other's parlors was a popular occasion, and an ideal one for exchanging gossip. An English traveler in Boston noted with some wit that "the ladies here visit, drink tea, and indulge in every little piece of gentility, to the height of the mode, and neglect the affairs of their families with as good a grace as the finest ladies in London."

More lavish entertainment at home included formal dinners, which often started in mid-afternoon. On such an occasion the hostess used her best china and crystal to show off a splendid menu of courses, which might comprise a choice of 20 different dishes, accompanied by various wines, beer, cider, and perhaps a rum or brandy punch. These were followed by an array of sweets— tarts, creams, custards, cakes—and then another dessert of fruits, nuts, and candies, often displayed at the center of the table in artistic pyramids. A large evening party, sometimes referred to ele-

gantly as a "rout," might include dancing and gambling to whet the appetite, after which the hungry guests sat down for supper by candlelight.

Music was a favorite pastime. Enthusiastic singers formed choral groups for singing part music, both in and out of churches. The wealthy and the not-so-wealthy attended concerts and recitals, and adults as well as children learned how to play the violin, spinet, or harpsichord.

TAKING TEA **This new social ritual brought new equipment into fashion.**

CULTURE PURSUED

Theaters were slow in getting started, particularly in Boston and Philadelphia, where plays were regarded as ungodly and corrupting, and were at first allowed only on the outskirts of town. Despite Quaker opposition, however, in 1754 a pioneering theater was built in Philadelphia (its backers arguing, somewhat illogically, that it was in a poor section and thus "no Nuisance would arise"). To get around prim prejudices in other

TAVERN STAPLE **Billiard tables were standard furniture in many taverns as well as private homes. This billiards game is taking place in a Maryland tavern. The cribbage board (inset), dating from 1735, is inlaid with the four suits of cards that were part of the game.**

COLONIAL BEST SELLERS

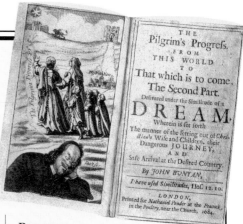

MOST OF THE BOOKS that were widely read in America in the 17th and 18th centuries were on religious or historical subjects, or else were books for children. Many of the earliest editions were published in London, with Boston and Philadelphia becoming publishing centers in the late 18th century.

The Pilgrim's Progress, by John Bunyan, was published in London in 1678. The allegorical story braces the protagonists' pilgrimage from "the City of Destruction to the Celestial City or The world that is to come." It was particularly popular in the New England colonies.

The Day of Doom, by Michael Wigglesworth, an American clergyman, was a religious book containing vivid images of the Bible.

The Tenth Muse Lately Sprung Up in America, a book of poems by Anne Bradstreet, was published in London in 1650. She was considered one of the first notable woman authors in America.

The Private Journal of a Journey from Boston to New York was written in 1704 by Sarah Kemble Knight. Madam Knight headed a Boston writing school, and her journals are rich with descriptions of everyday life in her era.

The Whole Book of Psalmes (better known as the *Bay Psalm Book*) was the first book published in America. It appeared shortly after

PERENNIAL CLASSIC The allegory of *The Pilgrim's Progress* drew a large reading audience for many years.

the first printing press was established in Cambridge, Massachusetts, in 1639.

Among the most lasting books for children were the celebrated *New England Primer* (1690), used in schools, and *The History of Little Goody Two Shoes* (1787).

cities, plays were often advertised under uplifting, if misleading, subtitles. Thus Shakespeare's *Hamlet* was billed as "a moral and Instructive Tale," and *Othello* as proof that "Happiness can only Spring from the Pursuit of Virtue."

Whether or not theatergoers required such reassurances, thespians were soon playing to packed houses from Charleston to New York, and new plays and leading actors became lively topics of conversation. With the writing of dramas by native-born as well as English authors, the American theater was on its way.

NATURE OBSERVED

Gardening—growing food and useful herbs—was a necessity for the earlier settlers, but toward the end of the 18th century an appreciation of the beauty of

THE PLAY'S THE THING Theater became increasingly popular throughout the 18th century, although its influence was often assailed by church groups. During the American Revolution performances were sometimes put on to raise funds for the war effort. When peace returned, touring theater companies visited every major city.

growing things—flowers, shrubbery, and trees—became an end in itself.

In the early days of the colonies, nature was regarded primarily as an enemy, as it was on the western frontier: a "hideous, howling wilderness" of forests, wild animals, and Indians that had to be cut down or otherwise subdued. Within the relative safety and comfort of cities, however, a realization of the basic beauties of nature began to emerge.

The colonists' growing fascination with nature and science was exemplified by John Bartram, a Quaker farmer who became known as the father of American botany, and his son William, a sensitive artist-naturalist who recorded many species of plants and animals native to the colonies that scientists had never seen before.

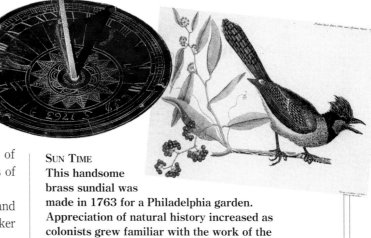

SUN TIME
This handsome brass sundial was made in 1763 for a Philadelphia garden. Appreciation of natural history increased as colonists grew familiar with the work of the naturalist Mark Catesby, who produced this etching of the crested jay after a journey through the South.

READING TIME
Mrs. William Frazier enjoys a book in this 1798 portrait of a gentlewoman at leisure.

As a result of their explorations, the Bartrams are credited with more than 200 plant discoveries, including new species of magnolias, rhododendrons, lilies, and phlox; the curious insect-eating venus flytrap; and, most notable of all, a small, lovely fall-flowering tree they found in Georgia and named *Franklinia altamaha* after their good friend Benjamin Franklin. (Fortunately they managed to save the seeds of the specimen they found, since the species has since disappeared completely from the wild.)

These and other horticultural rarities were coveted not only by connoisseurs in the colonies but were also shipped in regular consignments of seeds to eager gardeners and nurserymen in England, where exotic species from America were in constant demand. Perhaps the ultimate compliment to the plowman-turned-plantman, however, came from the famed Swedish classifier Carolus Linnaeus, who called John Bartram "the greatest living botanist in the world."

THE STRAIGHT AND NARROW
A wheeled "waywiser" rests in the corner of the potting shed bedecked with drying herbs at the Brush-Everard House at Colonial Williamsburg. The instrument was rolled along the ground to measure land plots and to keep the planting rows of a garden straight.

RIGORS OF CITY LIFE

For all their vitality, colonial cities were not always pleasant places in which to live.

Crime, foul smells and runaway horses were mere inconveniences

compared to early medical practices, which were as likely to kill as to cure.

AS CITIES GREW, peculiarly urban problems surfaced. Garbage disposal was primitive; slops and other refuse were simply thrown out in the gutter and left for dogs or hogs to consume. Water supplies and sanitation were rudimentary; city houses relied on backyard wells and outdoor privies—often located too close together for good health. Horse-drawn traffic was heavy, and frequently got out of control; to reduce chances of injury from runaways, pedestrians were separated from well-traveled streets by lines of stout, upright posts.

Of all city hazards, the one most feared was fire. It could start from a faulty chimney, a dropped candle, grease spilled on a stove—or an arsonist settling a personal grudge, a common practice in those days.

Most houses were built of wood with shingle roofs, at risk of burning because of the year-round use of chimneys for cooking; in many districts buildings were also crowded close together, so when a fire broke out it quickly spread. Moreover, without a ready supply of water from fire hydrants, there was little at hand to put it out. A devastating fire swept Boston in

MANHATTAN IN FLAMES   A disastrous fire almost totally consumed New York City in 1776, shortly after the British army forced the Americans to evacuate. British soldiers are shown here attacking citizens suspected of arson as others carry away valuables. The inaccurate blue uniforms are a late addition to the engraving.

1679, leaving 110 families homeless and many lives lost. In 1740, downtown Charleston went up in a blaze that consumed 300 homes as well warehouses and wharves. An even worse conflagration in 1776 destroyed a quarter of New York City before the fire could be brought under control.

To combat the menace, Boston, New York, Philadelphia, and other cities appointed fire wardens to check houses for potential hazards. They also established Mutual Fire Societies, volunteer companies that provided small, hand-pumped "water engines," ladders, and axes. But in many places fire fighters included every able-bodied man in town.

Hanging in the front hall of a responsible citizen's house was a pair of heavy leather fire buckets, marked with the owner's name or initials. At the dreaded cry of "Fire!" the man of the house, and his son if he had one, grabbed the buckets and ran to the reported site of the blaze; if he were delayed or away, his wife threw the buckets into the street so someone else could pick them up. Kept inside many buckets were canvas bags for salvaging valuables on behalf of the fire victims, and a "bed key" for dismantling an elegant master bed, which was often the most prized possession in a house.

At the scene of the fire, the volunteers of the bucket brigade formed two parallel lines from the house to the nearest source of water, usually a public pump, private well, pond, or stream. As each bucket was filled, it was passed up the "wet" line and thrown on the flames; the empties went down the "dry" line, often handled by boys, to be refilled at the source. When the fire had been extinguished, the buckets were placed in a pile so their owners could claim them and take them home, where they were kept ready for the next emergency.

Membership in a volunteer fire company was a matter of civic duty—among those who served in the ranks at one time or another were such famous Americans as George Washington, Thomas Jefferson, Samuel Adams, Alexander Hamilton, Paul Revere, and Benjamin Franklin (who was the founder of Philadelphia's Union Fire Company). It was also a matter of considerable pride. Like gentlemen's clubs, most companies met regularly, ostensibly for training but also for good fellowship. Some boasted lavishly decorated fire buckets, engines, fire horns, uniforms, and hats—not so much for fighting fires as for showing off at picnics, parades, ceremonial dinners, and competitions with rival companies.

VOLUNTEER **Benjamin Franklin wears the uniform of the Union Fire Company, one of the first volunteer fire-fighting outfits, which he founded in 1738.**

HAND PUMP **A 1792 water pump could project a stream of water up to 75 feet. It is similar to the one shown above in the Franklin portrait. At left above is a hand-sewn leather water bucket, of the kind taken to a blaze by volunteer firemen.**

CRIME AND PUNISHMENT

Among other problems, colonial cities provided fertile breeding grounds for social disorder and crime. Unlike small villages, where residents shared similar backgrounds and ideals, the larger ports were veritable stewpots of humanity—rich and poor, immigrants of various races and nationalities, sailors, drifters, vagrants, adventurers, confidence artists, and thieves. When the mix boiled over, it resulted in behavior that city fathers often deplored but could rarely keep under control.

FIRE MARK **Metal fire marks affixed to the outside of 18th-century buildings showed that the house and its contents were insured. This 1794 fire mark was on the wall of a Philadelphia house.**

RUN away, the 23d of this Inftant *January*, from *Silas Crifpin* of *Burlington*, Taylor, a Servant Man named *Jofeph Morris*, by Trade a Taylor, aged about 22 Years, of a middle Stature, fwarthy Complexion, light gray Eyes, his Hair clipp'd off, mark'd with a large pit of the Small Pox on one Cheek near his Eye, had on when he went away a good Felt Hat, a yelowifh Drugget Coat with Pleits behind, an old Ozenbrigs Veft, two Ozenbrigs Shirts, a pair of Leather Breeches handfomely worm'd and flower'd up the Knees, yarn Stockings and good round roe'd Shoes. Took with him a large pair of Sheers crack'd in one of the Bows, &c mark'd with the Word [*Savoy*]. Whoever takes up the faid Servant, and fecures him fo that his Mafter may have him again, fhall have *Three Pounds* Reward befides reafonable Charges, paid by me *Silas Crifpin.*

From a Philadelphia newspaper

ESCAPED
A reward is offered for information leading to the return of an indentured tailor's assistant.

In all cities, the most common offense was ordinary stealing. Hogs and chickens disappeared with great regularity, usually under cover of night. A gentleman foolish enough to leave his horse in front of an inn for a moment often returned to find the saddle and bridle gone—if not the horse. Pickpockets and shoplifters were everywhere. In Philadelphia, one woman was apprehended in the act of receiving a stolen silver porringer from her eight-year-old son, whom she had carefully taught the trade of Oliver Twist.

The gentry, whose wealth and aristocratic airs were especially resented, were favorite targets of burglary and vandalism. In Boston it was reported that "some wicked and evil minded Persons" had broken into

Governor Dummer's coach house and smashed the "Front Glass of his Chariot," and that others "stole a necessary house out of the Garden of Nathaniel Wardwell, Chaise-Maker, and carried it away." What they proposed to do with a used outhouse is not known.

Though constables and night watchmen might stroll the streets, there were no organized police forces, and a fast-moving culprit usually got away. In many cities, it was popular to attribute unsolved crimes, including serious ones, to British convicts, some 30,000 of whom were deported from England and sold as indentured servants in the colonies, saving the Crown the cost of maintaining them at home.

Even more feared by intolerant city dwellers were native Indians and blacks, either slaves or freed men, who formed a sizable fraction of the population of cities like New York. Because of their status, and the fear that they might revolt at any time, they were often dealt with more brutally than other suspects—rounded up at the slightest provocation, whipped for minor infractions, and sometimes put to death for crimes that called for a lesser penalty among whites.

Punishment for crimes was as immediate as possible, and was designed both to humiliate an offender

---

EYEWITNESS

CONVICTS—A GIFT FROM KING GEORGE

66 When we see our papers fill'd continually with accounts of the most audacious robberies, the most cruel murders, and infinite other villainies perpetrated by convicts transported from Europe, what melancholy, what terrible reflections it must occasion! What will become of our prosperity? These are some of thy favours Britain. Thou art called our Mother Country; but what good mother ever sent thieves and villains to accompany her children; to corrupt some with their infectious vices and murder the rest? What father ever endeavour'd to spread a

plague in his family?...In what can Britain show a more sovereign contempt for us by emptying their jails into our settlements; unless they would likewise empty their jakes [privies] on our tables!99

From *The Virginia Gazette*, 1751.

DEPORTED Found guilty of perjury, Elizabeth Canning was sentenced to seven years of indentured servitude in the colonies. The penalty turned out to be a blessing, giving her an opportunity to start over in Philadelphia.

PUBLIC HANGING   Executions drew huge throngs in the 18th century. The death penalty was imposed for crimes of murder, sodomy, witchcraft, and insurrection.

and to discourage others from attempting the same. Whipping continued to be common for a wide range of misdemeanors; so was forcing convicts to wear letters sewn onto their garments to advertise their crimes: "A" for adulterer, "B" for burglar, "D" for drunkard. Capital punishment was automatically imposed for murder, rape, and other major crimes.

DEBTOR'S CELL
The jail at Williamsburg, built around 1701, gives an idea of the misery of 18th-century imprisonment in this reconstruction of a debtor's cell. The boxlike structure in the corner is a toilet. A 1770 woodcut from a children's book, showing a thief being caught after stealing from a butcher, carries the warning "Honesty is the Best Policy."

Except for detaining a suspect while awaiting trial, imprisonment was generally avoided; it was considered a waste of money and manpower to keep people under guard and idle for any length of time at public expense. Those who did see the inside of a colonial jail, however, seldom forgot it. Men, women, and children, murderers, vagrants, and those of unsound mind were thrown indiscriminately together under miserable, crowded conditions, with poor food and barely room to sleep on the floor. Jails were often crammed into former private houses or the basements of public buildings. Some were so run-down, and security so spotty, that many inmates were able to escape.

Following the Revolution, the erratic and generally barbaric state of justice came under review, as reformers called for a more humane criminal code in keeping with the new U.S. Bill of Rights. Led by Dr. Benjamin Rush, a prominent physician and signer of the Declaration of Independence, a group of leading Quakers formed the Philadelphia Society for Alleviating the Miseries of Public Prisons.

The ideas of these pioneers were put into practice in 1790 at the city's newly remodeled Walnut Street Jail, where inmates were segregated by sex and by the nature of their crimes, were encouraged to be "penitent" through hard labor and meditation, and actually received small payments for their work. This first "penitentiary" was the beginning of an organized prison system in the United States.

TRIALS OF MEDICINE

Disease, the bane of the early settlers, became more widespread in the 18th century. In cities, crowding and poor sanitation led to epidemics, spread by large populations of rats, mosquitoes, and flies among the residents unaware of the relation of their illnesses to filth. A variety of "unruly distempers" could cut a terrible swath, from smallpox and typhoid fever to scarlet fever and whooping cough. Particularly insidious were "malignant fever," or influenza, which ravaged the colonies periodically, and diptheria, which led to

A RADICAL EXPERIMENT AGAINST SMALLPOX

DESPITE THE RUSTIC state of health care, the 18th century did see some notable progress on the medical front. The most significant took place in Boston in 1721, when a smallpox epidemic broke out. Cotton Mather, the fiery Congregationalist minister—who had lost five family members to a measles epidemic eight years before—heard news of successful small-

pox inoculations in Turkey, in which pus from a victim was applied to a small cut in an uninfected person's arm, causing a mild version of the disease.

Mather persuaded a physician in Boston, Zabdiel Boylston, to initiate an experiment in fighting this most dreaded of colonial diseases, against which there was no known protection at the time. Immediate objections came from other doctors, clergymen, and the public at large.

MEDICAL BREAKTHROUGH An account of Boylston's experiment was published in London in 1726.

A homemade bomb was thrown into Mather's home with the message, "Cotton Mather: you Dog, Damn you, I'll inoculate you with this, and a Pox to you!"

But 287 Bostonians were bold enough to volunteer. While more than half of the city's population fell ill with smallpox, and 15 percent died, the mortality rate among those inoculated was only 2 percent. It was the first successful immunization program in Western medicine, though the true causes and control of smallpox and other diseases would not be understood for at least another century and a half.

An Historical

ACCOUNT

OF THE

SMALL-POX

INOCULATED

IN

NEW ENGLAND,

Upon all Sorts of Persons, *Whites, Blacks,* and of all Ages and Constitutions.

With some Account of the Nature of the Infection in the NATURAL and INOCULATED Way, and their different Effects on HUMAN BODIES,

With some short DIRECTIONS to the UNEXPERIENCED in this Method of Practice.

Humbly dedicated to her Royal Highness the Princess of WALES, by *Zabdiel Boylston,* Physician.

LONDON:

Printed for S. CHANDLER, at the Cross-Keys in the Poultry. M.DCC.XXVI.

the deaths of about 5,000 persons, mostly children, in 1735-37, in New England alone.

In those days, Americans could be forgiven for dreading the doctor as much as the disease. As late as the 1770's, no more than one in 20 of those who practiced medicine in the colonies actually held an M.D. degree. The rest were persons with scant training who had set themselves up as physicians, apothecaries, or healers of various kinds. Most surgeons were barbers who supplemented their incomes from haircutting by lancing boils, setting broken bones, treating wounds, and amputating limbs—without anesthetics, antiseptics, or any creditable rate of healing success.

One New Yorker in 1757 complained that

HERBS AND POTIONS The 18th-century apothecary, often the closest thing that a community had to a physician, dispensed potions made mostly of herbs. This shop, with a skeleton to suggest the proprietor's erudition, is at Colonial Williamsburg.

"Quacks abound like locusts in Egypt." Thomas Jefferson noted that a patient, treated according to the latest fashion, "sometimes gets well in spite of the medicine." He also observed wryly that when he saw three or more doctors gathered in one place, he looked upward in search of buzzards waiting for the kill.

Theories of illness varied. Early clergymen, who often tended to their parishioners' bodily as well as spiritual needs, felt that disease was ultimately caused

by sin, and was to be cured only by prayer and divine forgiveness. Others relied on the ancient notion that sickness occurred when blood and other bodily fluids, or "humors," had gotten out of balance, and that "bleeding and blistering, purging and puking" were the only ways to restore a natural state.

Bleeding, to rid the body of hot, fever-producing liquid, was done by applying bloodsucking leeches to the flesh, or by opening a vein and letting the blood flow until a sufficient amount was thought to have been withdrawn. Since some prescriptions called for draining more blood than exists in the human body, it is no wonder that the technique often eliminated the patient's life along with the disease.

A local infection or injury was "blistered" with a caustic substance to produce a discharge from the skin. To rid the body of humors, emetics were administered to induce vomiting, or a strong laxative was used. Among the latter the most common was calomel, which was highly toxic in large doses, adding mercury poisoning and an eventual loss of teeth to the patient's other complaints. Not much better was a common prescription for the "miserable distemper known as the griping of the guts"—swallowing one or more bullets made of lead.

The popularity of many kinds of sweets, combined with a lack of toothbrushes and oral hygiene, forced most colonists to go through life with decaying and often painful teeth, not to mention bad breath. An English visitor wrote that even young American women were "pittifully Tooth-shaken" (a condition Benjamin Franklin ascribed to the eating of frozen apples and hot soup).

To ease a toothache, remedies ranged from a stiff jolt of brandy to the application of "brimstone and gunpowder compounded with butter, rub the mandible with it, the outside first being warmed." Drilling and filling were not yet practiced; the only cure was extraction. The job might be performed by a barber-sur-

EAR TRUMPETS These primitive hearing aids were included in Benjamin Bell's *Handbook of Surgery*, published in 1791.

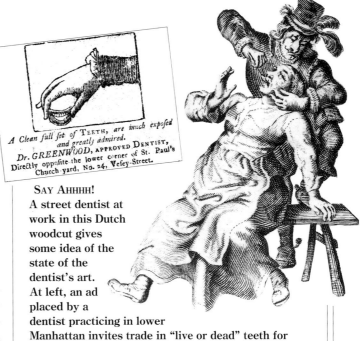

A Clean full set of TEETH, are much exposed and greatly admired.
Dr. GREENWOOD, APPROVED DENTIST,
Directly opposite the lower corner of St. Paul's Church-yard, No. 24, Vesey-Street.

SAY AHHHH!
A street dentist at work in this Dutch woodcut gives some idea of the state of the dentist's art. At left, an ad placed by a dentist practicing in lower Manhattan invites trade in "live or dead" teeth for the manufacture of false sets.

geon, a jeweler, or a blacksmith—or by a family member who tied a string to the offending molar and gave it a jerk. Such operations, along with more progressive dental care, and crude sets of false teeth carved out of wood, gradually came to be provided by professional dentists.

In early colonial days, anyone who became sick simply stayed at home, where relatives plied him with herb teas and other traditional remedies and lent him moral support. Martha Washington, who had lost several family members to tuberculosis, prescribed "capon ale," a hot chicken soup mixed with strong beer. If medically ineffective, it at least would give a patient a warm feeling in the face of death.

Some poorhouses maintained small infirmaries for inmates; the first true hospital in America was not opened until 1751. Backed by Benjamin Franklin, and financed mainly by private funds, Philadelphia's Pennsylvania Hospital accepted paying patients, charity cases, and the insane. In 1765 the first medical school was established at the College of Philadelphia, followed in 1767 by one at King's College (later Columbia University) in New York, and in 1783 by Harvard Medical School. Despite the availability of such training, most physicians had to serve seven years of apprenticeship under an experienced physician before being certified to practice on their own.

MARVELS OF TECHNOLOGY

Americans in colonial times benefited from progress in everything from housing

and transportation to the clothes they wore. When the economy became truly robust,

life was further improved with the institution of a national banking system.

I N SETTLING the New World, colonial farmers and "mechanicks" had long displayed a knack for adopting and improving upon any promising idea. A simple but striking example was the ax, the settlers basic tool for clearing forests, making building materials, and splitting firewood. By the 1700's, the heavy lopsided model inherited from England had been transformed into a lighter, balanced instrument with a broader blade and curved handle that enabled a practiced woodsman to fell three times as many trees in the same amount of time.

To convert logs into lumber, small operators built thousands of sawmills, taking advantage of the abundant waterpower available along North America's streams. Waterwheels drove the steel-edged blades that replaced handsaws to turn out huge quantities of planks and boards.

COTTON GIN The hand method of extracting seeds from cotton bolls ended when Eli Whitney invented the "gin" (short for engine). The machine (below) drew the bolls through teeth to separate out the seeds, and could deseed up to 15 bales a day.

The era also witnessed the beginnings of prefabricated housing. As early as the 1720's, a Philadelphia carpenter was selling standardized window frames, already painted and fitted with glass, for installation by homeowners. Another carpenter advertised precut, seasoned timbers ready to be assembled into houses 20 feet wide and 44 feet long. Toward the end of the century, nail-making machines replaced the crude process of forging nails individually by hand, helping to bring housing within everyone's reach.

Other inventors had an even greater impact on the development of American industry. Among them was a Delaware farm boy named Oliver Evans, who in 1782 designed an automatic gristmill, the first to mass produce flour. Evans's ideas, which he promoted in a best-sell-

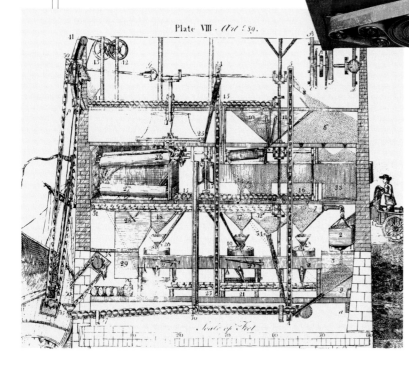

AHEAD OF ITS TIME Oliver Evans's ingenious automatic gristmill required the work of only one operator. Despite its efficiency, millers did not trust the design, and it failed to catch on.

ing handbook called *The Young Mill-Wright and Miller's Guide,* were soon pirated by others who, in the absence of patents, neglected to pay him any royalties.

Evans's greatest dream was to create a wagon driven by steam. He devised a compact and economical high-pressure engine that was very advanced for its time. Harnessed to a dredge in the Philadelphia harbor, it astonished spectators as it wallowed about like a prehistoric monster, pulling up buckets of mud, but was never an economic success. Nevertheless, Evans continued to dream. "The time will come," he told a friend, "when people will travel in stages moved by steam engines, from one city to another, almost as fast as birds fly, 15 or 20 miles in an hour . . . They [will] travel by night as well as by day; and the passengers will sleep in these stages." Oliver never lived to see the railroads that would unite the country and make his dream come true.

Two far-reaching developments affecting Americans' daily lives were related to making cloth. In 1789, Samuel Slater, a 21-year-old English textile worker, emigrated to New York. Hearing that Moses Brown, a wealthy Rhode Island merchant, was trying to mass produce cotton thread, Slater went to Pawtucket and rebuilt Brown's water-powered mill according to his detailed memory of designs already in use in England.

OUR INVENTIVE FOUNDING FATHERS

AMERICA'S LOVE AFFAIR with innovation embraced all segments of society. One celebrated gadgeteer was Thomas Jefferson, who, for a respite from politics, often turned his inquisitive mind to practical pursuits. An avid amateur architect, he designed such innovative structures as the University of Virginia in Charlottesville and the classic state capitol of Virginia in

BIFOCALS Franklin had the clever idea of combining lenses for near and distant vision in a single set of frames.

Richmond, as well as his own home at Monticello, for which he created storm windows, swinging French doors, revolving shelves, and a swiveling armchair, as well as a dumbwaiter used to bring up wines from the cellar.

Jefferson also tested new crops and applied innovative farming techniques to his fields at Monticello; he designed a portable three-legged camp chair which collapsed into a walking stick, invented a decoding machine, and contrived a device that used linked pens to make instant copies of his vast correspondence for his files.

Another famous innovator was Benjamin Franklin, who, in addition to his celebrated Franklin stove, pioneered the use of bifocal eyeglasses. As an outcome of his electrical experiments, which included flying a kite in a thunderstorm, he introduced the lightning rod, which proved its worth when lightning struck Franklin's own home.

STORMY INSIGHT Ben Franklin tied a key to a kitestring to prove lightning was linked to electricity.

FRANKLIN STOVE The efficiency of home heating was greatly improved by Franklin's innovations in stove design.

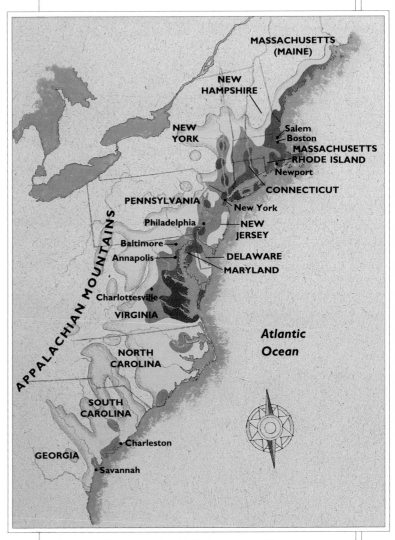

STATE MONEY These coins and bills were the standard currency in New Jersey before the national banking system was established in 1791.

Slater's Mill, as it was to be known, was the first successful spinning mill built in the United States and the beginning of the textile industry that later dominated the life of many towns throughout New England.

In 1792, young Eli Whitney, who was studying law in Savannah, Georgia, heard local planters complaining that they could not grow cotton profitably because of the time it took to clean. Within a year Whitney had created a hand-cranked device that moved raw cotton through a series of saw-toothed wheels, wire slots, and brushes to remove the seeds. This gin, which could clean as much cotton in a day as 50 workers could do by hand, was soon in such demand that Whitney could not make enough of them in the factory he opened in Connecticut.

Near the end of the 18th century, the raw materials that the new United States provided were greatly in demand overseas: grain, meat, leather, wool—and, after the invention of the cotton gin, especially cotton. Foreign trade was so robust that by 1790 the value of U.S. imports and exports—43 million dollars—had more than tripled in 30 years. An organized banking system became imperative. The colonists had been plagued by currency shortages and wide fluctuations in the value of paper money. English pounds and shillings, French sou, and Spanish pistoles and doubloons were all in circulation, in addition to colonial coins and paper currency.

After the Revolutionary War, colonial currency was almost worthless because of the new nation's wartime debt. The situation led to the phrase "not worth a Continental," still occasionally heard today. In the 1780's, the first American banks were founded (the Bank of North America, in Philadelphia in 1781, and the Bank of New York and the Bank of Massachusetts in 1784). These early banks held savings deposits, made loans, and issued their own paper money—largely backed by public confidence in the owners.

In 1791, the first national bank, the Bank of the United States, was chartered in Philadelphia, finally giving the new nation a sound dollar. This, in turn, gave all merchants, manufacturers, workers, and farmers the incentive to follow the injunction of the first U.S. penny: "Mind your business."

COLONIAL GROWTH By 1750 there were 13 separate colonies along the East Coast; Maine was then part of Massachusetts. By the time of the first census, in 1790, only six cities (Philadelphia, New York, Boston, Charleston, Baltimore, and Salem) had more than 8,000 people. Shading shows the growth of settlements up to 1660, in 1700, and in 1760.

TOWARD A
NEW NATION

1788 PARADE BANNER OF THE NEW YORK SOCIETY OF PEWTERERS

Inflamed by a policy of "taxation without representation,"

rebellious colonists launched the American Revolution against the British monarchy.

The war pitted brother against brother and produced more than

six years of hardship and suffering, on the home front as well as on the battlefield.

To the world's surprise, the colonists won—and gained the unprecedented

right to live their lives as a free people.

RISING RESENTMENT

As tensions escalated, pressure mounted on individual colonists to choose

sides. Patriots harassed suspected loyalists, who were forced to flee or fight back,

and groups began preparing to defend themselves.

THE 13 COLONIES were living in peace and relative prosperity when Britain unwittingly lit a fuse. Beginning with the Stamp Act of 1765, Parliament increasingly aggravated the colonists by trying to impose taxes without their consent. In reaction outraged colonists—lawyers, businessmen, journalists, and others—formed the Sons of Liberty, secret organizations in many towns where plans were made for resisting British officials, and patriotic demonstrations increased. In 1770 street gangs provoked British soldiers to fire into a crowd, an incident that became infamous as the Boston Massacre; three years later leading citizens in Boston, angered about the tea tax, organized the Boston Tea Party, disguising themselves as Indians to board ships in Boston Harbor and dump chests of tea into the sea. In 1775, when Massachusetts colonists fired on red-coated British soldiers trying to capture their military stores at Lexington and Concord, the stage was set for war.

As the momentum grew, many Americans (including Thomas Jefferson) still hoped for a reconciliation with the mother country. But on January 10, 1776, the fuse

BOSTON TEA PARTY Colonists disguised as Indians threw chests of tea off a British ship into Boston Harbor in 1773, an event that helped bring the debate between Tories and patriots to the level of fervor shown at left in an argument taking place in a New England meeting house. In 1776 the publication of Thomas Paine's *Common Sense* proved equally inflammatory, selling 100,000 copies between January and June.

TAR AND FEATHERS

IN PROTEST
A tarred and feathered customs official is forced by colonists to drink tea in this British cartoon.

66 There was great excitement in the country against the British ministry, and the newspapers were filled with pieces against them to keep the feelings of the people against taxation and other oppressions real and imaginary. All the feelings were against the British and there was very few of these called Tories.

In one instance and the only one that took place in York County was an attempt to tar and feather a young Dutchman [German] for venturing to give an opinion with respect to the times at a house raising…. The young man was one of these called Menonists [Mennonites] spoke against mustering and told them that the day would come when they would repent it…. The committee pronounced him an enemy to his country and a Tory and that he should be tarred and feathered. Some busy person had sent a tarbox such as is used for wagons, and a boy had a pillow of feathers. The young man was ordered in front of the courthouse where the tarbox was standing, but no one was there to tar him. One of the committee, a very violent man, said he must tar himself. The young man pulled off his shirt and put one hand in the tarbox and applied it to his shoulder, when the boys interfered and told him to let the person who ordered him to take up his shirt and jacket and go home…. Some mischievous persons ripped up the pillow and shook the feathers after him. I was witness to the whole proceedings until I saw the boys leave him, and so ended a very foolish and ridiculous affair…. I have no doubt that if the boys had joined in the business and feathered the poor man there would have been more of it. But to their everlasting credit they put the business down at once. 99

**From the memoirs of
Private John Adlum of the York
(Pennsylvania) Militia, 1776.**

reached the powder keg. Thomas Paine published his impassioned *Common Sense*, a pamphlet which exhorted its readers: "Everything that is right or reasonable pleads for separation. The blood of the slain, the weeping voice of nature cries, 'Tis time to part.'"

The cry of freedom, written in simple and direct language, reached ordinary people, who could read but were not well educated, in a way that the rhetoric exchanged by the elite had so far not done. Copies of the document sold from New Hampshire to Georgia, and were read by men and women along country roads as well as in the streets.

But as their convictions became clarified, people were under increasing pressure to take sides. Perhaps a third of Americans openly espoused the patriot cause, while another third remained loyal to the Crown; the rest were uncommitted, unsure, or unwilling to risk their lives. Neighbors, friends, and families faced wrenching divisions. While Benjamin Franklin led the opposition, his son William, the governor of New Jersey, remained a loyalist through his arrest and imprisonment, and was disinherited by his father in his will.

People who did not declare themselves as patriots were harassed by those who did. Roving bands threatened people suspected of Tory leanings or rumored to have made remarks against the rebel cause, and even pillaged their households. Loyalists were accused of being "traitors in our midst" and subjected to confiscation of property or worse—some were tortured, whipped, and driven from town tied to a wood railing, giving rise to the phrase, "ridden out of town on a rail;" some were also hung.

Many loyalists sought safety behind the British lines. Close to 100,000 fled to Canada or to England; others decided to stay and fight. In the course of the war an estimated 30,000 to 50,000 men

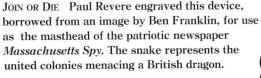

JOIN OR DIE Paul Revere engraved this device, borrowed from an image by Ben Franklin, for use as the masthead of the patriotic newspaper *Massachusetts Spy*. The snake represents the united colonies menacing a British dragon.

joined pro-British military units such as the King's American Regiment and the Queen's Rangers. Promised sanctuary, thousands of black slaves deserted their masters to supply labor for the English forces in the South; like Northern blacks who sided with the patriots, some fought as soldiers as well. In the Continental Army many New England companies included African-American soldiers. The First Rhode Island Regiment was 80 to 90 percent black, although all officers were white.

PREPARING FOR CONFLICT

When news of the Battle of Lexington reached Pomfret, Connecticut, it is said that Israel Putnam, who was to become one of General Washington's great citizen-generals, was plowing his fields. He calmly unhitched his horse, the story goes, summoned the local militia to follow him, and rode 100 miles directly to Boston to command the Battle of Bunker Hill. In actuality, the colonies' preparations for war were far more complex. Longstanding militia units had become primarily social rather than military organizations. Some were called Minutemen because of their supposed ability to assemble quickly at the signal of an Indian attack, but most had grown rusty for lack of practice. In the early days of the war, men were armed mostly with what they could bring from home. These rifles, or hunting weapons called fowling pieces, could not be fitted with bayonets, and the military-issue smooth-bore miscuits (also used by the British) that were available had an effective range of only 75 yards. General Washington's quartermaster general, a Rhode Island iron founder named Nathanael Greene, was a resourceful administrator, but he was faced with an almost impossible task due to the shortage of weapons, ammunition, and other supplies. Most of the gunpowder initially had to be imported from Europe, though some states were able to make their own—when they could find enough sulfur and saltpeter, or potassium nitrate, to do the job.

Connecticut, which prided itself on its nickname "the provisions state," provided the military with a steady supply of beef, grain, and cheeses, and also persuaded gunsmiths to increase their production of suitable weapons with a bounty of five shillings per gun. Even more important was the conversion of iron foundries to produce badly needed cannon. Foundries at Salisbury and Lime Rock, Connecticut, in particular are credited with many of the pieces used by the Continental Army and Navy, as well as the production of the round shot, grape shot, and canister with which they were armed. From these and other forges also came musket barrels, bayonets, sabers, anchors, chains, camp kettles, and a host of tools and fittings needed by armies and warships on the move. Hillsides from Connecticut southward to Virginia glowed day and night with the red glare of charcoal mounds and furnaces that transformed the raw materials of hardwood and red earth into the weapons of war.

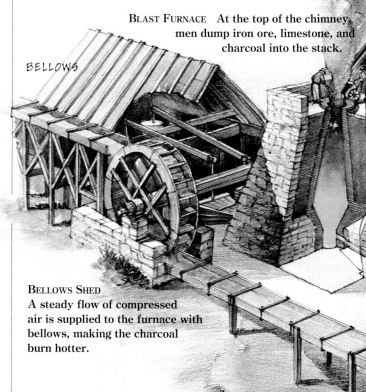

BLAST FURNACE   At the top of the chimney, men dump iron ore, limestone, and charcoal into the stack.

BELLOWS

BELLOWS SHED
A steady flow of compressed air is supplied to the furnace with bellows, making the charcoal burn hotter.

WAR EFFORT   Iron ore, limestone, and charcoal—all necessary for the smelting of iron—were in rich supply near Salisbury Connecticut, where the first foundry was built in 1748. In January 1776, blacksmiths, iron molders, and builders began to upgrade the forge for the manufacture of cannon, needed for the war effort, and some employees were made exempt from military service. Men kept the furnace stoked night and day. If fuels were not evenly supplied, the half-melted ore "froze up" in a lump called a "salamander"; then workers would have to dismantle and clear the chimney before it could be refired. By late 1778 the foundry had produced more than 800 cannon for the Continental Army and for privateers preying on British ships. The workers' furnace store (above right) no longer remains but the house of the ironmaster still stands.

IRONMASTER'S HOUSE

FURNACE STORE

CHARCOAL HOUSE
Fresh-made charcoal is
stored near the furnace
to assure a steady
supply.

BORING MILL After
cooling, the solid
barrel casting is
moved to the boring
mill and lowered,
muzzle down, onto a
rotating drill. This
tedious process may
have led to the
modern meaning of
the term "boring."

DEEP MOLDS The furnace is tapped,
allowing the white-hot iron to drain
across the casting floor. A movable
trough directs it into the deep pit
of sand holding cannon molds
buried upright with the mouths
at ground level.

CANNON MOLDS

BARREL
CASTINGS

123

THE PEOPLE GO TO WAR

Armed conflict was grim, especially when food and supplies were scarce. Women were not insulated from the war—some helped out on the battlefields, others replaced husbands and brothers in civilian jobs. Family life was further disrupted when soldiers were billeted in private homes.

AS MILITIA UNITS were called up and a Continental Army was formed, it seemed unlikely that a ragtag collection of farmers and shopkeepers could face the hardened British regulars with much hope of success. Most men who showed up for service, whether drafted or as volunteers, were poor young men who had been laborers, landless farmers, or apprentices; some arrived as paid substitutes for men of wealthy families, and some were slaves. Virtually all were poorly equipped, knew nothing about battle tactics, were unaccustomed to discipline, and were reluctant to spend time away from their homes and farms, especially as the war dragged on and conditions grew worse. Even George Washington had his doubts about the enormity of the task, admitting candidly that his job was "too boundless for my abilities and far, very far beyond my experience." Nevertheless, with grim determination—and the help of a few professional soldiers like the famed Prussian drillmaster Baron Friedrich von Steuben—

LOG VILLAGE By the time Washington's army camped near Morristown, New Jersey, in December 1779, the majority of the men were veterans of two to three years of battle. Here the soldiers use peacetime skills to build a village of log huts, 14 feet by 16 feet, to house 12 enlisted men each. Officers' huts housed up to four men.

A CRUEL WINTER AT MORRISTOWN

66 No man could endure [the storm's] violence many minutes without danger of his life...some of the soldiers were actually covered while in their tents and buried like sheep under the snow.... We are greatly favored in having a supply of straw for bedding. Over this we spread our blankets, and with our clothes and large fires at our feet, while four or five are crowded together, preserve ourselves from freezing. But the sufferings of the poor soldiers can scarcely be described. While on duty they are unavoidably exposed to all the inclemency of storms and severe cold. At night they now have a bed of straw on the ground and a single blanket to each man. They are badly clad and some are destitute of shoes. 99

WINTER SOLDIER This Continental Army rifleman is armed with a "Brown Bess," the smooth-bore musket the Americans were always pleased to capture from British soldiers.

Dr. James Thacher, Continental Army surgeon, January, 1780.

officers whipped their raw recruits into staunch military units that could deliver massed musket fire and stand up to, or mount, a bayonet charge.

While their men went off to war, women were far from idle. Many wives had to take over their husbands' duties at home, running farms, taverns, printing presses, or artisans' shops. Daughters of Liberty, who had organized before the war to observe British boycotts by weaving homespun cloth to use in place of British textiles, and by refusing to drink British tea, took more active roles. The largest wartime organization of women was The Association, founded in Philadelphia and led for a while by the daughter of Benjamin Franklin, Sarah Franklin Bache. Members were active in six states, raising money, weaving, sewing, and knitting clothing for the troops. Other women's groups collected blankets, mended uniforms, rolled bandages, prepared saltpeter for gunpowder, or melted down lead from window sash weights to cast into musket balls.

A number of women wrote eloquently about patriotic duty, in poems or broadsides that were widely distributed. More than one patriotic lady used her comings and goings by horse and carriage to observe the movement of enemy troops and reported valuable information to the rebel side. Some women even showed up on the military front themselves. Many wives were unwilling to be separated from their husbands; other women, wives and widows, became refugees after their homes or farms were destroyed by the British, leaving them with no means of support. As camp followers they earned their keep by cooking, washing clothes, mending uniforms and stockings, and performing various other chores. During battles they helped overburdened army

SOLDIER HUTS Wooden bunks are stacked three to a wall in the huts reconstructed at Morristown National Historical Park, where 10,000 soldiers were encamped during the worst winter of the war. Soldiers cooked their own meager rations on the hearth in their huts or in tent camp kitchens. Iron braziers like the one at right were available only for the use of officers.

MOLLY PITCHER Women served in battle by carrying water to gun crews for damping down cannon barrels after each firing. Mary Hays McCauley, pictured above, earned the nickname Molly Pitcher when she took up her husband's position.

doctors by tending the wounded and trying to nurse them back to health. General Washington considered camp following a liability, and urged his officers to keep it to a minimum, observing that "the multitude of women…especially those who are pregnant, or have children, are a clog upon every movement." Nevertheless, the commander, always concerned about having enough food for his army, allotted half rations for the women and quarter rations for each child.

Washington's own wife, Martha, was one of several officer's wives who joined their husbands in the winter encampments, where top officers were quartered in private homes. Martha arrived at her husband's headquarters in a coach loaded with hams, jellies, and

REDCOATS IN NEW YORK The British army parades through New York City shortly after taking it over in September 1776. The city became a Tory stronghold during the occupation, which lasted seven years. More than 4,000 captured Continental soldiers and patriots were imprisoned there in makeshift jails, churches, warehouses, and rotting ships.

A SOLDIER'S LETTER HOME

66 Friends, the ladies here are slender, of erect carriage and plump without being strong.

They have small and pretty hands and arms, a very white skin, a healthy color in the face... with no need for cosmetics. I have seen few disfigured by pockmarks, for inoculation

SCARLET CLOAK
These brilliant cloaks were popular with both men and women.

against smallpox has been in vogue for many years. They frizz their hair everyday and gather it up in the back of their head into a chignon and puff it up in the front.

In the English colonies the beauties have fallen in love with red silk or woolen wraps. Dressed in this manner, a girl will run, walk or dance about you and bid you a friendly good-morning or give you a saucy laugh...sometimes roguishly offering us an apple accompanied by a little curtsy.

Nearly all activities necessary for the adornment of the female sex are at present either very scarce or dear, and for this reason they are now weaving their Sunday finery. Should this begin to show signs of wear, the husbands will be compelled to make their peace with the Crown if they will keep their women-folks supplied with geegaws. **99**

A Hessian mercenary, fighting for the British, marched through Connecticut after the British defeat at Saratoga in 1777.

other comforts from home, and stayed for weeks, during which she would occasionally pay visits to the soldiers along their rows of tents or barracks, where the men would set up a cheer for "Lady Washington."

A few petticoat patriots actually fought alongside their men. The most famous of these was an Irish lass named Mary who accompanied her husband, a young artilleryman from Pennsylvania, to spend the grim winter of 1777-78 at Valley Forge, then marched with the troops to New Jersey, where they met the British in the Battle of Monmouth on a blistering day in June. Dubbed Molly Pitcher because of her tireless efforts to bring water to the gun crews, for swabbing out the barrels of the cannon as well as slaking the thirst of the soldiers under bombardment, she stepped in to load the cannon when her husband collapsed from the heat. In his autobiography, Private Joseph Martin recalled a dramatic moment:

"While in the act of reaching [for] a cartridge and having one of her feet as far before the other as she could, a cannon shot…passed directly between her legs without doing any other damage than carrying away all the lower part of her petticoat. Looking at it with apparent unconcern, she observed that it was lucky it did not pass a little higher…and continued her occupation."

THE WAR COMES HOME

Civilians often tasted the harsh realities of war. Many who lived near areas of battle were forced to billet sol-

diers or officers in their homes, often at the peril of their daughters and wives. Others were stripped of livestock, wagons, clothes, food, rum, and anything else deemed useful in waging war. In several Connecticut towns, the *New London Gazette* reported, British and Hessian mercenary troops fighting with them "entered the houses, attacked the persons of Whig and Tory indiscriminately, breaking open desks, trunks, chests, closets, and taking away everything of value; they robbed women of buckles, rings, bonnets, aprons, and handkerchiefs."

Anti-British feelings were further inflamed by stories of Indians enlisted by the English who appalled even the most hardened military officers by shooting and scalping settlers and plundering their homes. News of one such atrocity spread quickly through the colonies. The victim was a young woman named Jane McCrea, the daughter of a

FRONTIER SCALPING
Continental Army enlistments soared after the murder of Jane McCrea by Iroquois allies of the British.

TRIALS OF ARMY LIFE

BEYOND THE TERROR and pain of occasional battles, perhaps the most striking aspects of the Revolution were the unrelentingly brutal conditions that soldiers were forced to endure.

For the Continental Army, food, clothing, blankets, and other necessities were always in short supply, as were guns, ammunition, wagons, and horses needed to face the enemy. At Washington's encampment at Valley Forge in the winter of 1777–78, more than two-thirds of his troops were barefoot or wearing strips of blankets or rawhide around their feet in place of shoes. The Marquis de Lafayette, a French soldier and statesman who fought on behalf of the Americans, described their terrible plight: "The unfortunate soldiers were in want of everything; they had neither coats, hats, shirts nor shoes; their feet and legs froze until they became black, and it was often necessary to amputate them."

BATTLEFIELD SURGERY Clockwise from the top are an amputation knife, bullet extractor, surgical scissors, multibladed lancet, and a trepanning device used for treating head wounds.

Even foraging parties came up with little; the surrounding countryside had long since been looted of livestock, grain, and firewood. To relieve his men's misery, Washington dispatched urgent pleas to various governors of the new states. Jonathan Trumbull of Connecticut replied by rounding up 300 head of cattle from local farmers, and had them driven on the long overland trek to Valley Forge. Within five days of the arrival of the herd every animal had been devoured. The leader of the cattle drive, Colonel Henry

Champion, observed that the beef had been picked over so thoroughly, "you might have made a knife out of every bone."

Under such circumstances, it is little wonder that thousands fell victim to exposure, malnutrition, and disease. Field hospitals, described as "houses of carnage," were primitive and unsanitary, without sufficient doctors, nurses, or medicines. Patients were mixed indiscriminately on dirty straw mats in huts and tents, so that typhus and other fevers spread among the wounded. One physician reported that he had "known four or five patients to die on the same straw before it was changed."

On top of it all, military pay was low and unreliable; for months at a time, men were not paid at all. At Valley Forge, the dirgelike chant went up among soldiers huddled around their fires: "No meat, no clothes, no pay, no rum."

Nevertheless, loyalty to the army grew. In 1778, when the French supplied the Continental army with red-trimmed uniforms in both brown and blue, the soldiers resisted wearing the non-traditional brown uniforms. A lottery was held and the losing regiments were forced to accept the brown uniforms, which became known as "lottery coats."

MEDICINE CHEST A portable physician's case of the Revolutionary War era suggests how little medical aid a doctor could give. Because germs were not understood, it held no disinfectants.

MEDICAL AID A doctor bandages a wounded soldier in a brown "lottery coat." A patient facing surgery was lucky to get a glass of brandy to ease the pain. Most literally bit on a bullet.

BRITISH SURRENDER The regimental flag of the Philadelphia Light Horse Troop and a Continental signal drum flank the scene of Continental troops, by this time a skilled fighting force, lined up with French regiments and naval units as the British army prepares to surrender to George Washington following its defeat at Yorktown in October 1781.

minister who, ironically, was engaged to a loyalist lieutenant in the army of General Burgoyne. Abducted near Fort Edward in upper New York, she was carried off with another woman into the woods, where a violent argument erupted among her captors.

According to a witness, "In the midst of the fray, one of the Chiefs in a rage shot Jenny McCrae in her breast, & she fell & expired immediately…. The same chief took off [her] scalp…. He then sprang up, tossed the scalp in the face of a young Indian standing by, brandished it in the air, and uttered a savage yell of exultation." The image of the young woman's long blond hair, dripping blood, provided a powerful piece of propaganda to the rebel cause.

In areas not directly affected by the fighting, life proceeded as normally as it could. The cutoff age for boys expected to render military service was 16, and most children who attended school continued as usual. Colleges like Yale and Harvard were disrupted, however, by the departure of students enthusiastic to fight for either the rebel or the loyalist side. Shortages in goods no longer available from England were endured with a sense of patriotic purpose. Churches in most towns continued to hold regular services, though the ministers and members of some Anglican parishes were hounded by self-appointed patriots who questioned their colonial loyalties, to the point where some were forced to shut down until the end of the war.

Whatever ultimately turned the tide of battle—rebel determination, English lack of enthusiam for the war, French intervention and support, or a combination of blunders and pure luck—the Continentals rallied from early disasters, endured the terrible shortages of food and equipment, and grew from an army of inexperienced youths into well-trained troops, until their opponents were ready to call it quits. In the process the patriots experienced something more profound than victory. They discovered that they were no longer just Virginians, or Pennsylvanians, or New Yorkers, divided by provincial rivalries. United in blood and freedom, they were now Americans all.

INTO A NEW CENTURY

The mood of the newly independent nation was ebullient

as it set about planning and leading a life of its own.

WITH THE WAR finally ended, owners of farms and factories could turn their attention to pouring out increasing volumes of raw produce and finished goods which merchants were free to trade without restrictions. Ship captains who had harassed the enemy as privateers turned to a booming peacetime business, opening up new trade routes to Europe and the Orient and laying the foundation for a growing merchant marine. Fresh waves of immigrants arrived to seek their fortunes under the Stars and Stripes, and many of them began to move westward over the Appalachians to settle the nation's expanding frontiers.

Noting the key statement in the Declaration of Independence that "all men are created equal," and that many blacks had served with distinction in the war, abolitionists renewed efforts begun earlier to put an end to slavery. In 1783 the Supreme Court of Massachusetts outlawed the practice in its state. The next year Thomas Jefferson's proposal to ban the holding of slaves in new U.S. territory was only narrowly defeated, though eight decades would pass before that terrible issue was settled once and for all.

Meanwhile, the new fascination with freedom and politics led to spirited campaigns and elections at all levels of government—including the

SYMBOLIC EAGLE This early version of the Great Seal of the United States was sketched in 1782 by Secretary of Congress Charles Thomson.

stirring speeches and victory celebrations that became the trademarks of American democratic life. In 1789 a new Constitution was adopted and George Washington, promptly elected by a grateful nation, took the oath of office as President of the United States, with his capital originally in New York and then in Philadelphia.

The first national census, carried out the next year, showed that the new country had just under four million citizens. To provide them with a new seat of government on the banks of the Potomac, Washington accepted the services of Pierre Charles L'Enfant, a young French architect and engineer, who laid out the federal city that would bear the great hero's name. By 1800, the newly built White House was deemed ready enough for President John Adams to move in (Mrs. Adams emphatically disagreed, observing that "the great

HAIL TO THE CHIEF Washington's arrival in New York City for his inauguration as first president of the new republic in 1789 is shown as a triumphant event in this romantic rendering.

POLITICAL BARBECUE   The 1800 public cookout depicted by Lewis Miller was held "on the common open ground" at York, Pennsylvania, to celebrate the election of Thomas McKean as governor of the state. The feasting and parade of local military companies helped lay the groundwork for an American political tradition.

unfinished audience room" was the only place she was able to hang up her laundry to dry).

By the inauguration of the third president, Thomas Jefferson, the eyes of the nation were turned increasingly toward the West. Kentucky was admitted as a state in 1792, Tennessee in 1796. To provide the clamoring residents of these states and the bustling Ohio Valley with a trading outlet direct to the ocean, Jefferson made an offer to buy the port of New Orleans from France.

To his astonishment—and nearly everyone else's—Napoleon replied by offering to sell the entire territory lying west of the Mississippi that the French and Spanish called Louisiana. For a mere $15 million, the United States doubled the size of its holdings in a single stroke of a pen, and set the stage for the next era of colonization— all the way to the California coast.

LOUISIANA PURCHASE
An 1819 map describes the "Immense Territory" of Louisiana, "obtained by purchase from the French… without one drop of blood being shed." At right, the United States flag is raised in New Orleans on the occasion of the takeover of the 909,000 square miles of the Louisiana Territory, doubling the young nation in size.

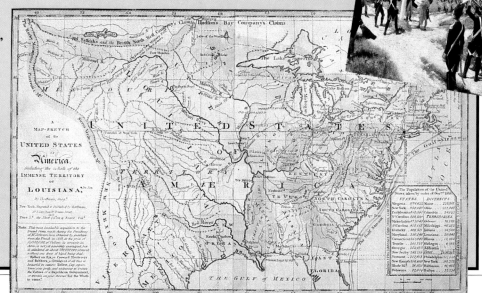

THE WAY IT WAS: SELECTIONS FROM DAILY LIFE

FRENCH COLUMN One of the earliest attempts at North American settlement was made by French Huguenots in 1562, on the coast of what is now South Carolina. The colony was soon abandoned but the settlers left behind a stone column bearing the coat of arms of the King of France. Two years later an Indian chieftain guided the leader of another French expedition to the site, where tribesmen were found treating the column as a shrine. Expedition artist Jacques LeMoyne made this sole surviving painting.

NATIVE AMERICANS OBSERVED
Some of the finest early views of flora, fauna, and native peoples of North America come from the sketches and watercolors of John White, a leader of Sir Walter Raleigh's ill-fated Roanoke Colony. These images, made in the summer of 1587, appeared the following year as engravings in *A Briefe and True Report of the New Found Land of Virginia,* published in London by Thomas Hariot.

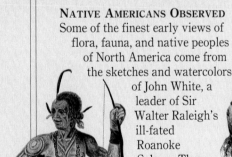

TOBACCO—THE CASH CROP
The Jamestown settlers tried their hand at such diverse ventures as prospecting, glassblowing, and winemaking before finding the crop that brought success to the colony—tobacco. In 1613, John Rolfe crossed local tobacco with a West Indian strain, producing a superior variety that found a ready market in England. By 1619, Jamestown was sending almost 50,000 pounds of tobacco across the Atlantic each year. The colony's tobacco boom might have gone bust in 1621, when England's King James, a fierce foe of smoking, tried to get Parliament to ban the importation of tobacco. The London businessmen who sponsored the colony, however, convinced the lawmakers to table the proposed law and keep Jamestown profitable.

CLOSED HELMET
The "closed helmet" (with a face guard) was worn by a man-at-arms on guard at Wolstenholme Town, a small hamlet established a few miles from Jamestown in 1620. Two years after its founding the settlement was one of many sites assailed in a widespread Indian uprising throughout Virginia. More than half the settlers died, all homes were burned to the ground, and the town was never rebuilt. In the 18th century the land was part of the grandiose estate, Carter's Grove, and the town's remains were not unearthed until the 1970's. The helmet is one of only two examples of such armor ever found in English America.

MAIZE—THE SAVING CROP
Tobacco brought economic salvation to Britain's southern colonies, but it was corn, or maize, first cultivated by the Indians, that kept settlers alive in both Virginia and New England. The crop fed both people and livestock, and it required less time and effort to cultivate than other grains.

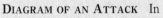

DIAGRAM OF AN ATTACK In 1637, tensions between Pequot Indians and settlers in Connecticut boiled over after the Indians killed white traders. Puritans retaliated by destroying a Pequot village with the aid of Indian allies, shown in the outer ring of this engraving of the attack.

1640 – 1700

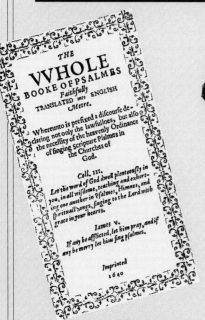

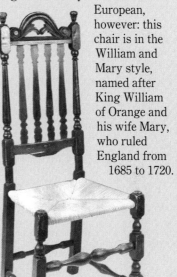

A HANDSOME NEW ENGLAND CHAIR By the late 17th or early 18th century, when this bannister-back chair was put together by a Connecticut craftsman, most furniture was made in the colonies rather than imported from England. The styles were still European, however: this chair is in the William and Mary style, named after King William of Orange and his wife Mary, who ruled England from 1685 to 1720.

WHAT'S NEW—THE FIRST BOOK PRINTED IN AMERICA In 1640, the year after Stephen Daye set up the first printing press in New England in a "cow-yard" adjoining newly-founded Harvard College, Daye's press printed the first book published in the United States. *The Whole Booke of Psalmes Faithfully Translated into English Metre,* better known as *The Bay Psalm Book,* was widely used for many years. Today only 11 copies are known to have survived.

PURITAN GARB
Puritans observed a double standard in their apparel. In New England, as in Old England, dress was seen as a reflection of social class; in the Bay Colony, sumptuary laws permitted leading citizens to wear finery such as gold lace, while prohibiting "excess apparel" for less prosperous or distinguished colonists.

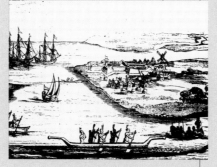

FORBIDDEN PLEASURES
Puritan leaders banned such "popish" customs as the observance of Christmas, or other holidays they considered pagan, but colonists sometimes risked the wrath of the clergy by indulging in lighthearted pastimes—for example, celebrating the arrival of spring with a dance around the maypole.

NEW AMSTERDAM PLAN
The first view of the New World city founded by the Dutch did not appear in print until 1651. The drawing from which it was made was an earlier work, possibly done by the engineer sent from Holland to lay out the streets. The houses and the mill are thought to be accurate, but the fort never reached the size the planner imagined here.

THE COLLEGE OF WILLIAM AND MARY Higher education came to the southern colonies with the founding of William and Mary at Williamsburg, Virginia, in 1693. Plans under way since 1618 were delayed after the Indian uprising of 1622. In the early years most students there intended to be ministers. The first purely secular institution of higher learning in the country was Philadelphia College, later the University of Pennsylvania, established in 1755.

1 7 0 0 – 1 7 4 0

COLONIAL WARS Colonial America was not a peaceful place.

Even during relatively quiet periods, farmers kept their muskets in easy reach while working their fields, and all able-bodied men served in local militia units. Conflicts with the Indians over land encroachments were aggravated by territorial competition among the English, French, and Spanish for domination of North America. The Pequot War, and King Philip's War, fought in New England from 1675-1678, are two periods of conflict covered by Samuel Penhallow, an English-born merchant who became both a judge in New Hampshire and an important early historian of the colonies. His valuable account of Indian wars in New England was published in 1726.

SURVEYING NEW ORLEANS
The French advance down the Mississippi River and along the Gulf of Mexico led to the founding of New Orleans as a trading post in 1718. This engraving shows Jean Baptiste Le Moyne, Sieur de Bienville, laying out the colony. Most of the first citizens of New Orleans were hardy settlers lured south from Canada.

THE NATURAL HISTORY OF THE NEW WORLD English-born naturalist and artist Mark Catesby made two lengthy visits to the colonies in the first half of the 18th

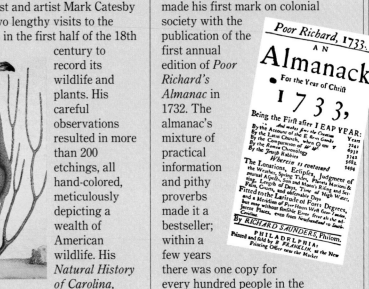

century to record its wildlife and plants. His careful observations resulted in more than 200 etchings, all hand-colored, meticulously depicting a wealth of American wildlife. His *Natural History of Carolina, Florida, and the Bahama Islands,* documenting three years of his travels, was published in London in 1731. Apart from his contribution to the natural sciences, Catesby awakened a new appreciation of their resources among many colonists.

ST. AUGUSTINE While English colonies spread along the Atlantic coast to the north, Spain held on to its stronghold in Florida. Although theoretically off limits to the British, the St. Augustine port was visited by British ships and British goods were welcomed, since Spanish goods were often in short supply.

WHAT'S NEW—POOR RICHARD'S ALMANAC Benjamin Franklin made his first mark on colonial society with the publication of the first annual edition of *Poor Richard's Almanac* in 1732. The

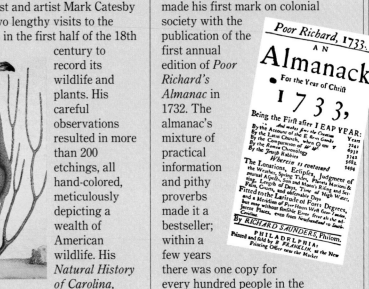

almanac's mixture of practical information and pithy proverbs made it a bestseller; within a few years there was one copy for every hundred people in the colonies.

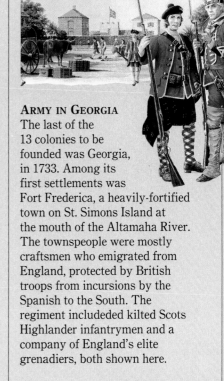

ARMY IN GEORGIA
The last of the 13 colonies to be founded was Georgia, in 1733. Among its first settlements was Fort Frederica, a heavily-fortified town on St. Simons Island at the mouth of the Altamaha River. The townspeople were mostly craftsmen who emigrated from England, protected by British troops from incursions by the Spanish to the South. The regiment includeded kilted Scots Highlander infantrymen and a company of England's elite grenadiers, both shown here.

1740 – 1760

SURVEYOR'S COMPASS

Surveyors played an important role in colonial America. In New England, growing communities appointed surveyors to set boundaries and lay out lots in new townships. In the South, where the constant need for more tobacco land made speculation in frontier real estate a profitable enterprise, surveyors were often the first white colonists to penetrate the wilderness beyond the Tidewater. One such pioneering surveyor was young George Washington. In 1748, the wealthy Lord Fairfax, a neighbor and distant relative, hired the sixteen-year-old Virginian to survey some of his immense property west of the Blue Ridge Mountains. Washington performed so well that he was made surveyor of Culpeper County the following year. This is the magnetic compass Washington used in his surveying expeditions.

FINE SEWING Ladies who did fancy needlework took up the popular flame-stitch pattern, using wools dyed in several colors to make chair seats, pillow covers, and panels for firescreens like this one, to set before an open hearth as a decorative accent calling attention to an imposing fireplace. The screen could be moved up and down the pole to keep the heat from the fire off the faces of those seated in front of it.

HOSPITAL RECORDS

A page from the early records of the first hospital in the colonies, established in Philadelphia in 1752, lists admissions, ailments, and the results of treatment. In spite of the primitive state of medicine at the time, and the constant threat from epidemic disease—especially smallpox—colonists generally led healthier and longer lives than most of their European counterparts.

	Admitted.	Cured.	Relieved.	Irregular Behaviour.	Incurable.	Taken away by their Friends.	Dead.	Remaining.
AGUES	3	3	—	—	—	—	—	1
Cancer,	3	2	—	—	—	—	2	—
Colliquative Purging,	2	—	—	—	—	—	—	—
Consumption,	1	1	—	—	—	—	—	—
Contusion,	1	1	—	—	—	—	—	—
Cough, of long standing,	9	4	1	—	1	—	3	—
Dropsies,	2	1	1	—	—	—	—	—
Empyema,	3	2	—	—	—	2	—	—
Eyes disordered,	2	2	2	—	1	—	—	1
Falling Sickness,	3	1	—	—	—	—	—	—
Fevers,	3	2	—	—	—	—	—	—
Fistula in *Ano*,	1	1	—	—	—	—	—	—
in *Perinæo*,	1	1	—	—	—	—	—	—
Flux,	1	1	—	—	—	—	—	—
Gutta Serena,	1	—	—	—	—	—	—	—
Hair Lip,	1	1	—	—	—	—	—	—
Hypocondriac Melancholy,	18	2	3	—	4	6	1	3
Hypopyon,	1	—	—	—	—	—	—	—
Lunacy,	1	1	—	—	—	—	—	—
Mortification,	1	—	—	—	—	—	—	—
Prolapsus *Ani*,	1	1	—	—	—	—	—	—
Uteri,	1	—	—	—	—	—	—	1
Palsy,	6	—	6	—	—	—	—	2
of the Bladder,	1	—	—	—	—	—	—	1
Rheumatism and Sciatica,	6	6	1	1	2	—	3	3
Scorbutick and scrophulous Diseases,	9	21	4	2	1	—	3	—
Ulcers, with Caries, &c.	37	1	—	—	—	—	—	—
Vertigo,	1	1	—	—	—	—	—	—
Uterine Disorder,	1	—	—	—	—	—	—	—
Wen,	1	—	—	—	—	—	—	—
Wounded,	1	—	—	—	—	—	—	—
In all,	117	60	11	3	7	10	10	16

BRADDOCK'S DEFEAT

In the summer of 1755, the colonies were rocked by news of the defeat of the British General Edward Braddock in an ambush by French troops and their Indian allies along the Monongahela River. For much of the 18th century, colonists lived with war and rumors of war as England and France struggled to gain control over New World turf. After 1763, when the Treaty of Paris brought peace and an end to French claims in Canada, the colonists grew increasingly independent, feeling less need for defense by British troops. The shift in attitude helped to prepare the way for colonial rebellion.

TOBACCO EXPORTS BOOM

Tobacco was the mainstay of the colonies along Chesapeake Bay throughout the 18th century. The labor-intensive crop fueled the growth of slavery; in 1756, Virginia had about 120,000 slaves out of a population of 290,000.

PEOPLE ROUSER Paul Revere was a well established artisan and engraver by 1770 when the Boston Massacre occurred. His engraving of the event, skewed against the British, and inaccurate in any case, was a remarkably successful piece of propaganda.

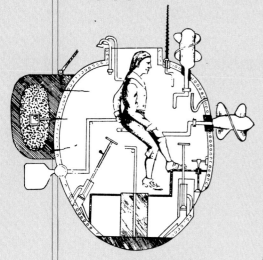

YANKEE INGENUITY Sergeant David Bushnell of Connecticut designed and built the world's first military submarine in 1775. The hand-operated vessel failed in an attempt to sink several British warships in New York Harbor the following year.

ROYAL PROCLAMATION

After the first shots betwen colonial minutemen and British troops were fired at Lexington on April 19, 1775, the painful separation of the colonies from the mother country was spelled out in a number of documents over the next year. On August 23, 1775, King George III issued his proclamation "for suppression of rebellion and sedition," shown below, following the "olive branch" petition, drawn up by members of the Second Continental Congress.

Written in appeasing language, the petition was actually intended to provoke the king, and to persuade reluctant colonists that their only choice was to rebel. When the document reached England, the king refused to receive it, demonstrating the royal intractability that led Thomas Paine to label him "the royal brute of England" five months later in his inflammatory pamphlet *Common Sense*. The next July the direction of the colonies was set by the finest document of all, the Declaration of Independence.

BROTHER AGAINST BROTHER

Some families in the British colonies were divided between those loyal to the crown and advocates for rebellion. Pennsylvania's famed inventor-statesman, Benjamin Franklin, a staunch patriot, disinherited his son William, who was then the governor of New Jersey, and a Loyalist. In Millerton, New York, John Holley, Jr., joined a Continental regiment and fought in the Battle of Saratoga while his brother Newman Holley joined the British Light Infantry, a Loyalist unit. Here are recruiting posters for the First Battalion of Pennsylvania Loyalists and the Continental Army's 11th regiment.

1 7 7 6 — 1 8 0 3

FIRST FLAG The first flag design of the rebellious colonies, featuring 13 stripes to represent the 13 colonies and a British Union Jack in the corner, suggests the ties still binding the colonists to England. The more familiar design, above, which replaced the Union Jack with 13 stars, was adopted by the Continental Congress on June 14, 1777. This version was flown by the *Andrew Dovia* in 1776, when it received the first salute recognizing the United States as a sovereign state in a Dutch port in the Caribbean.

FINEST FASHION
Once the Revolutionary War was over, those Americans with the time and money to follow fashion again looked to Europe for inspiration. Stylish citizens eagerly awaited ships bearing samples of the latest in clothes from London and Paris; a few days after the ships arrived, local milliners, dressmakers, and tailors would have copies in their shops available for sale.

QUACK DOCTORS Cartoons remained a favorite outlet for expressing British-American antipathies after the war. One easy target for satire was an invention by a Connecticut doctor, Elisha Perkins, that used metal wedges "to draw off the noxious electrical fluid that lay at the root of suffering." When the device was patented in England this cartoon appeared, ridiculing the instrument "just arrived from America—Perkinism in all its glory, being a certain cure for all disorders—Red Noses, Gouty Toes, Windy Bowels, Broken Legs and Hump Backs." U.S. doctors also tried to discredit the invention, but it made Perkins a wealthy man.

SPANISH CALIFORNIA
The war that ended the colonial status of settlements in the East was distant news in the string of Spanish missions along the California coast. This pen sketch is the earliest known view of Spanish California, made in 1786. The French explorer La Pérouse is being greeted by friars and Indians upon his arrival at San Carlos Borromeo de Carmelo, the second of the missions to be founded by Father Junipero Serra. All buildings shown were later replaced.

LEMUEL HAYNES
The hopes for liberty and equality aroused by the Declaration of Independence made few inroads in racial terms. One oustanding example was Lemuel Haynes, who

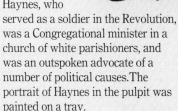

served as a soldier in the Revolution, was a Congregational minister in a church of white parishioners, and was an outspoken advocate of a number of political causes.The portrait of Haynes in the pulpit was painted on a tray.

FIRST IN WAR, FIRST IN PEACE
Admiring citizens of the young nation produced many tributes to their hero George Washington. From top to bottom the three items shown here are an idealized view of the surrender of Cornwallis to Washington that ended the war, an engraving depicting Washington's inauguration on the balcony of Federal Hall, and a fanciful painting of George and his wife, Martha, in the fraktur style of the Pennsylvania Germans.

PLACES TO SEE

Travelers in the United States have the opportunity to visit hundreds of restored historic villages, battlefields, houses, and museums that bring alive what daily life was like in Colonial America. Here is a selection of such places you can write for descriptive literature and further information.

THE NORTHEAST

MASSACHUSETTS

Boston National Historical Park
  (includes 9 historic sites)
  Charlestown Navy Yard
  Boston, MA 02129
Historic Deerfield, Inc.
  Hall Tavern Information Center
  Deerfield, MA 01342
Massachusetts Historical Society
  1154 Boylston Street
  Boston, MA 02115
Museum of Fine Arts, Boston
  465 Huntington Avenue
  Boston, MA 02115
Peabody Museum of Salem
  East India Square
  Salem, MA 01970
Minute Man National Historical Park
  P.O. Box 160
  Concord, MA 01742
Salem Maritime National Historic Site
  Custom House, Derby Street
  Salem, MA 01970
Old Sturbridge Village
  1 Old Sturbridge Road
  Sturbridge, MA 01566
Pilgrim Hall Museum
  75 Court Street
  Plymouth, MA 02360

1627 Pilgrim Village at Plimoth Plantation, Massachusetts

Plimoth Plantation
P.O. Box 1620
  Plymouth, MA 02360
Saugus Iron Works National Historic Site
  244 Central Street
  Saugus, MA 01906

18th-century chamber pot at Historic Deerfield, Massachusetts

VERMONT

Old Constitution House
  North Main Street
  Windsor, VT 05089

CONNECTICUT

Litchfield Historical Society
  South and East Streets
  Litchfield, CT 06754
Salisbury Cannon Museum
  Holley-Williams House
  Lakeville, CT 06039
Mystic Seaport Museum
  P.O. Box 6000
  Mystic, CT 06355
The Wethersfield Historical Society
  150 Main Street
  Wethersfield, CT 06019

RHODE ISLAND

The Preservation Society
of Newport
  118 Mill Street
  Newport, RI 02840
Slater Mill Historic Site
  Roosevelt Avenue
  Pawtucket, RI 02862
Roger Williams National Memorial
  282 N. Main Street
  Providence, RI 02903

NEW YORK

The Brooklyn Museum
  188 Eastern Parkway
  Brooklyn, NY 11238
The Farmers' Museum
  Route 80
  Cooperstown, NY 13326

Fraunces Tavern
  54 Pearl Street
  New York, NY 10004
Jean Hasbrouck Memorial House
  Huguenot Street at North Front Street
  New Paltz, NY 12561
Museum of the City of New York
  1220 Fifth Avenue
  New York, NY 10029
New York Historical Society
  170 Central Park West
  New York, NY 10024
South Street Seaport Museum
  207 Front Street
  New York, NY 10038
U.S. Military Academy
  Fort Putnam, Route 218
  West Point, NY 10996
Van Cortlandt Manor
  off NY 9A, South Riverside Avenue
  Croton-on-Hudson, NY 12534

Officer's gear at Morristown National Historical Park, New Jersey

NEW JERSEY

Morristown National Historical Park
  230 Morris Avenue
  Morristown, NJ 07960
Old Barracks Museum
  Barrack Street
  Trenton, NJ 08608

PENNSYLVANIA

American Swedish Historic Museum
  1900 Puttison Avenue
  Philadelphia, PA 19145
Bartram's Gardens
  54th Street and Lindburg Boulevard
  Philadelphia, PA 19109
Elfreth's Alley Association
  128 Elfreth's Alley
  Philadelphia, PA 19109
Ephrata Cloister
  2451 Kissel Road
  Lancaster, PA 17601

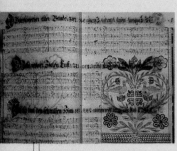

Sheet music at Ephrata Cloister, Pennsylvania

Fort Necessity National Battlefield
RD 2, Box 528
Farmington, PA 15437
The Franklin Institute Science Museum
20th and the Parkway
Philadelphia, PA 19103
Hopewell Furnace National Historic Site
Route 345
Elverson, PA 19520
Independence National Historical Park
313 Walnut Street
Philadelphia, PA 19106
Moravian Historical Society
214 East Center Street
Nazareth, PA 18064
Pennsylvania Farm Museum
of Landis County
2451 Kissel Road
Lancaster, PA 17601
Valley Forge National Historical Park
Valley Forge, PA 19481
Washington Crossing Historical Park
Route 32
Washington Crossing, PA 18977
York County Historical District
250 Market Street
York, PA 17043

DELAWARE

New Castle Historical Society
2 East 4th Street
New Castle, DE 19720
The Delaware State Museums
Meeting House Galleries I and II
316 South Governors Avenue
Dover, DE 19901

1716 Mons Jones House at American Swedish Historical Museum, Pennsylvania

Henry Francis duPont
Winterthur Museum
Winterthur, DE 19735

THE SOUTH

MARYLAND

Historic Annapolis Foundation
194 Prince George Street
Annapolis, MD 21401
Maryland Historical Society
201 West Monument Street
Baltimore, MD 21201

DISTRICT OF COLUMBIA

National Museum of American Art
8th and G Streets, N.W.
Washington, DC 20560
National Museum of American History
14th Street and Constitution Avenue, N.W.
Washington, DC 20560

VIRGINIA

The Claude Moore Colonial Farm
at Turkey Run
6310 Georgetown Pike
McLean, VA 22101

18th-century cooking at Colonial Williamsburg, Virginia

Colonial National Historical Park
P.O. Box 210
Yorktown, VA 23690
Colonial Williamsburg
P.O. Box 1776
Williamsburg, VA 23187-1776
Gunston Hall
Route 242
Lorton, VA 22121
Mount Vernon, Washington's Home
Mount Vernon Ladies' Association
Mount Vernon, VA 22121
Jamestown Settlement
P.O. Box Drawer JF,
Williamsburg, VA 23187
Valentine Museum
1015 East Clay Street
Richmond, VA 23219

NORTH CAROLINA

Fort Raleigh National Historic Site
Route 64-264
Manteo, NC 27954
Kings Mountain National Military Park
P.O. Box 40
Kings Mountain, SC 28086
Museum of Early Southern
Decorative Arts
924 South Main Street
Winston-Salem, NC 27101
Old Salem
Old Salem Road
Winston-Salem, NC 27108

KENTUCKY

Cumberland Gap National Historical Park
P.O. Box 1848
Middlesboro, KY 40965
Old Fort Harrod State Park
College Street
Harrodsburg, KY 40330

TENNESSEE

Jonesborough Historic District
117 Boone Street
Jonesborough, TN 67359
Frank H. McClung Museum
The University of Tennessee
1327 Circle Park Drive
Knoxville, TN 37996

SOUTH CAROLINA

Beaufort Historic District
Chamber of Commerce
910 Bay Street
Beaufort, SC 29902
The Charleston Museum
360 Meeting Street
Charleston, SC 29403

Chippendale bookcase at Heyward-Washington House, The Charleston Museum, South Carolina

Charleston Trident Visitors Bureau
P.O. Box 975
Charleston, SC 29402

Charles Towne Landing 1670
 1500 Old Town Road
 Charleston, SC 29407
Drayton Hall
 3380 Ashley River Road
 Charleston, SC 29414
Middleton Place and Gardens
 Route 61
 Charleston, SC 29407
Ninety-Six National Historical Site
 P. O. Box 496
 Ninety-Six, SC 29666

GEORGIA
Fort Frederica National Monument
 Route 9, Box 286-C
 St. Simons Island, GA 31522

FLORIDA
Fort Caroline National Memorial
 12713 Fort Caroline Road
 Jacksonville, FL 32225
Historic St. Augustine
 Chamber of Commerce
 1 Riberia Street
 St. Augustine, FL 32084

ALABAMA
Fort Conde
 150 South Royal Street
 Mobile, AL 36602

LOUISIANA
LSU Museum of Art
 Memorial Tower
 Baton Rouge, LA 70803
LSU Rural Life Museum
 6200 Burden Lane
 Baton Rouge, LA 70808
Louisiana State Museum
 P. O. Box 2448
 New Orleans, LA 70176

Magnolia Mound Plantation,
Louisiana

Magnolia Mound Plantation
 2161 Nicholson Drive
 Baton Rouge, LA 70802
Vieux Carré Commission
 516 Chartres
 New Orleans, LA 70112

THE MIDWEST

MICHIGAN
Henry Ford Museum
and Greenfield Village
 20900 Oakwood Boulevard
 Dearborn, MI 48124

OHIO
Schoenbrunn Village State Memorial
 State Route 259, East High Avenue
 New Philadelphia, OH 44663

MISSOURI
Great River Road Interpretive Center
 66 South Main Street
 St. Genevieve, MO 63670

ILLINOIS
Fort de Chartres
 Route 155
 Prairie du Rocher, IL 62277

INDIANA
Vincennes Mile of History
 417 Busseron Street
 Vincennes, IN 47591

MINNESOTA
Grand Portage National Monument
 P.O. Box 668, 315 South Broadway
 Grand Marais, MN 55604

THE WEST

TEXAS
San Antonio Missions National
Historical Park
 (includes 4 mission sites)
 2202 Roosevelt Avenue
 San Antonio, TX 78210

Spanish Governor's Palace
 105 Military Plaza
 San Antonio, TX 78205

NEW MEXICO
Chaco Culture National Historical Park
 Star Route 4, Box 6500
 Bloomfield, NM 87413

Mission Concepción, Texas

Pueblo of Acoma
 P.O. Box 309
 Pueblo of Acoma, NM 87034

ARIZONA
Tumacacori National Monument
 Box 67
 Tumacacori, AZ 85640
Mission San Xavier del Bac
 1950 W. San Xavier Road
 Tucson, AZ 85746

La Purisima, California

CALIFORNIA
La Purisima Mission State Historic Park
 2295 Purisima Road
 Lompoc, CA 93436
Mission Santa Barbara
 Upper Laguna Street
 Santa Barbara, CA 93105
Mission San Carlos Borromeo de Carmelo
 3080 Rio Road
 Carmel, CA 93923

Spanish chocolate cup at
National Historic Museum
of Los Angeles County,
California

INDEX

ACKNOWLEDGMENTS

The editors gratefully acknowledge the cooperation and counsel of the following institutions and individuals in the research for the text and appropriate images for this work. We are particularly indebted to many at Colonial Williamsburg—including Catherine Grosfils, Mary Keaton, and Pat Gibbs.

Also our gratitude goes to: **American Antiquarian Society**, Georgia Barnhill; **American Renaissance**, Mark Winter; **American Swedish Historical Museum**, Cindy Palmer; **Anglo-American Museum**, T. Ross Bacot; **Archivos de Indias**, Rosario Darra; **British Museum**, Paul Davis; **The Brooklyn Museum**, Karen Tates; **Brown University Library**, Peter Harrington; **Charleston Museum**, Mary Giles; **Charles Towne Landing 1670**, Janson Cox; **Chicago Historical Society**, Lorraine Mason; **CIGNA Museum**, Melissa Hough; **Colonial National His-**torical Park, Peggy Gaul; **Connecticut Historical Society**, Michelle Parish; **Corning Museum of Glass**, Jill Thomas Clark; Culver Pictures; **Elfreth's Alley Association**, Gail Petty; **Ephrata Cloister**, Nadine Smith; **Essex Institute/Peabody Museum**, Kathy Flynn; **Farmer's Museum, Inc.**, Kathleen Stocking; **Franklin Institute of Science**, Gladys Breuer; **Free Library of Philadelphia**, Karen Lightner; **Guilford Courthouse National Park**, Mark Woods; **Gunston Hall**, Mary Lee Allen; **Henry Ford Museum**, Dawn Johnston; **Historic Deerfield, Inc.; Historic Charleston**, Connie Wyrick; **Historic Hudson Valley**, Burns Patterson; **Historic Society of Delaware**, Annette Woolard; **Historic St. Augustine Preservation Board**, Susan Parker; **Historical New Orleans Collection**, John Magill; **Holland Society of New York**, Peggy Hutchinson; **Huntington Art Gallery**; **Independence National Historic Park**, Shirley May; **Jamestown Settlement**, Diane Stalling; **Landis Valley Museum**, Vernon Gunnion; **Library Company of Philadelphia**, Susan Ogama; **Library of Congress**, Bernard Reilly; **Litchfield Historic Society**, Jennifer DeSimas; **Los Angeles Natural History Museum**, John Cahoch; **Louisiana Historical Society**, Richard Bell; **Louisiana State Museum; LSU Rural Life Museum**, John Dutton; **Lynn Historic Society**, Ken Turino; **Magnolia Mound Plantation**, Lauren Young; **Mansell Collection Ltd.**, George Anderson; **Marblehead Historical Society**, Bette Hunt; **Massachusetts Historical Society**, Chris Steele; **McClung Museum**, Jefferson Chapman; **Mesa Verde National Park**, Art Hutchinson; **Metropolitan Museum of Art**, Beatrice Epstein; **Moravian Historical Society**, Susan Dreydoppel; **Morristown National Historical Park**, Joni Rowe; **Museum of Early Southern Decorative Art**, Brad Rauschenberg; **Museum of Fine Arts, Boston**, Mary Sluskonis; **Museum of New Mexico**, Willow Powers; **Museum of Science and Industry**, Marry Scareno; **Museum of the American Indian**, Laura Nash; **Museum of the City of New York**, Marguerite Lavin; **Mystic Seaport Museum**, Phillip Budlong; **National Gallery of Art**, Charles Richie; **National Park Services**, Wade Meyers; **New Netherland Project**, Dr. Charles Gehring; **New Orleans Public Library**, Sally Reeves; **New York Historical Society**, Diana Arecco; **N.Y. Public Library**, Wayne Furmay, Ted Teodoro; **Newberry Library**, Rebecca Weiss; **Ohio Historical Society**, Gary Arnold; **Old Salem**, Johanna Metzger; **Old Sturbridge Village**, Meg Haley; **Philadelphia Museum of Art**, Tamatha Kuehz; **Pictorial History Research**, Bob Wahlgren; **Pilgrim Society**, Peggy Timlin; **Plimoth Plantation**, Peter Cooke, Pat Baker; **Rhode Island Historical Society**, Linda Eppich; **Rhode Island Museum of Art**, Mellody Enuis; **Rocky Hill Historical Society**, Anita Watson; **Salem Maritime National Historical Site; Salisbury Cannon Museum**, Whitney N. Seymour, Jr.; **San Antonio Missions National Park**, Roslyn Rock; **Saugus Iron Works Nat'l Historical Site**, Carl Simons; **Shelburne Museum Inc.**, Pauline Mitchell; **Society for the Preservation of New England Antiquities**, Tracy Hodgson; **Society of Antiquaries**, Adrian James; **University of California, Berkeley**, Richard Ogar; **Valentine Museum**, Teressa Roane; **Valley Forge National Historical Park**, Bob Dotson; **Virginia Museum of Fine Arts**, Howell W. Perkins; **Winterthur Museum**, Bill Seltzer; **York County Historical Society**, Janet Deranian.

PICTURE CREDITS

AAS American Antiquarian Society; **CM** Cigna Museum; **CW** Colonial Williamsburg; **DP** Dover Publications; **HNOC** Historic New Orleans Collection; **LC** Library of Congress; **MAHS** Massachusetts Historical Society; **MDHS** Maryland Historical Society; **MFA** Museum of Fine Arts, Boston; **NG** National Gallery of Art; **NL** Newberry Library; **NLM** National Library of Medicine; **NPS** National Park Service; **NYHS** New York Historical Society; **NYPL** New York Public Library; **OSI** Old Salem, Inc.; **PC** Personal Collection; **PHR** Pictorial Historical Research; **WM** Henry Francis duPont Winterthur Museum; **YCHS** York County Historical Society

Read from top to bottom of page, left to right:

1 LC. 2 MFA. 4 Archivos de Indias; Metropolitan Museum. 5 LC; CW; NYHS (2). 6 LC; NPS. 7 LC; McClung Museum. 8 LC; LA Natural History Museum. 9 AAS. 10 YCHS. 11 Archivos de Indias. 12 *Illus:* Steven Patricia. 13 James Quine (2); Florida State Archives 14-15 *Illus:* Dahl Taylor. 15 Pat Lods. 16 LC. 17 PC; Bill Ballenberg; Hubert Lowman. 18 Mark Winter (2). 19 Museum of International Folk Art. 20-21 *Illus:* Steven Patricia. 21 PC. 22 *Illus:* Dahl Taylor; Ken Barrett, Jr., Historic St. Augustine. 23 LC. 24 NPS. 25 LC; CW. 26 LC; British Museum. 27 NYPL (2); LC. 28 NPS. 29 *Background:* NYHS; Pilgrim Society (2). 30 National Museum of the American Indian; PC; History Today. 31-33 *Illus:* Steven Patricia (2). 33 *Illus:*

Dan Rutter. 34 *Illus:* Steven Patricia. 35 CW (3); WM. 36 NYPL (2); MFA. 37 *Illus:* Lauren Jarrett. 38 Essex Museum. 39 First Congregational Church/Woodstock, CT; Paul Rocheleau; Connecticut Historical Society; Rocky Hill Historical Society 40 New Haven Colony Historical Society 40 *Illus:* Dahl Taylor. 41 Historic New Orleans Collection. 42-43 *Illus:* Steven Patricia. 43 LC. 44 NPS. 45 Museum of the City of New York; MFA. 46 WM. 47 LSU Rural Life Museum. 48 Historic New Orleans Collection. 49-50 NL (2). 51 *Illus:* Dahl Taylor. 52 New Orleans Notarial Archives (2). 53 *Illus:* Steven Patricia. 54 *Illus:* Dan Rutter; *Illus:* Dahl Taylor. 55 CW. 56 Museum of the City of New York. 57 *Illus:* Steven Patricia. 58 Brooklyn Museum; *Background:* Brooklyn

Museum; PC. 59 *Illus:* Dan Rutter (2); PC. 60 NY State Historical Association 61 American Swedish Historical Museum. 62 *Illus:* Dan Rutter (2); Essex Museum. 63 *Background:* NYPL; Moravian Historical Society 64 Ephrata Cloister. 65 MDHS; *Illus:* Steven Patricia. 66 YCHS; OSI. 67 Old Salem, Inc. (3); Corning Museum. 68 *Illus:* Dahl Taylor; NG.69 The Metropolitan Museum. 70 *Background:* LC; Connecticut Historical Society 71 PHR; MAHS; LC; PC. 72 Philadelphia Museum of Art. 73 Christies NY; LC; CW (2). 74 CW; NY State Historical Association 75 CW; LC. 76 CW; LC. 77 Connecticut Historical Association; Museum of Early Southern Decorative Arts. 78 PC; NG; CW. 79 NYPL; YCHS. 80-81 Charles Baptie/Gunston Hall; NPS. 82 CW (2); AAS. 83 MDHS; LC. 84-85

Charleston Museum; *Illus:* Steven Patricia. 86 NPS. 87 Valentine Museum; Landis Valley Museum (2); Museum of Science and Industry. 88 Charleston Museum; CW. 89 Culver Pictures. 90 LC. 91 Landis Valley Museum (2); NG. 92 MDHS; *Illus:* Dahl Taylor. 93 NYHS. 94 *Background:* CM; Elfreth's Alley Association 95 LC (2). 96 Lynn Historical Society 96-97 NPS. 97 DP. 98 Peabody Museum; Marblehead Historical Society 99 *Background:* MDHS; Old Sturbridge Village; DP. 100 NPS; LC. 101 *Illus:* Steven Patricia. 102 Washington and Lee Univ.; MFA; CW. 103 WM; CW; Library Company of Philadelphia. 104 CW (2); AAS. 105 MAHS; CW (2); MAHS. 106 Pilgrim Society 107 WM; CW (2); MDHS. 108 LC (2). 109 CW; LC; Historical Society of Delaware; CW. 110 LC.

111 CM (4). 112 PHR; CW. 113 LC (2); CW. 114 LC; CW. 115 PHR; LC; NLM (2). 116 LC; Smithsonian Institution; LC. 117 NPS; LC; PC. 118 NPS; *Illus:* Dahl Taylor. 119 NYHS. 120 LC (3); 121 DP; LC. 123 *Illus:* Steven Patricia. 124 NPS. 125 NPS (3). 126 LC (2); 127 CW; LC. 128 NPS (3). 129 *Background:* LC; NPS (2). 130 National Archives; NYHS. 131 YCHS; *Background:* LC; Louisiana Historical Society. 132 NYPL; LC (3); CW; Jamestown Foundation. 133 LC (3); NYPL; PC (2). 134 LC (6); NPS. 135 Smithsonian Institution; PC; Historical Society of Wisconsin; LC; Pennsylvania Hospital. 136 LC (3); DP; NYPL. 137 Daughters of American Revolution; CW; LC (3); University of CA/Berkeley; Museum of Art/Rhode Island School of Design; CW.